PUFFIN

Don't let your secrets fall into enemy hands! Learn to write your secret messages in code using your mobile phone, crossword puzzles, paperclips and lemon juice. They are ingenious, baffling and great fun!

For Catherine

Crack the Code

K WOODWARD

PUFFIN

PUFFIN BOOKS

Published by the Penguin Group
Penguin Books Ltd, 80 Strand, London WC2R 0RL, England
Penguin Group (USA) Inc., 375 Hudson Street, New York, New York 10014, USA
Penguin Books Australia Ltd, 250 Camberwell Road, Camberwell, Victoria 3124, Australia
Penguin Books Canada Ltd, 10 Alcorn Avenue, Toronto, Ontario, Canada M4V 3B2
Penguin Books India (P) Ltd, 11 Community Centre, Panchsheel Park,
New Delhi – 110 017, India
Penguin Books (NZ) Ltd, Cnr Rosedale and Airborne Roads, Albany, Auckland,
New Zealand
Penguin Books (South Africa) (Pty) Ltd, 24 Sturdee Avenue, Rosebank 2196, South Africa

Penguin Books Ltd, Registered Offices: 80 Strand, London WC2R 0RL, England

www.penguin.com

First published 2004
1

Set in Stone Sans

Made and printed in England by Clays Ltd, St Ives plc

British Library Cataloguing in Publication Data
A CIP catalogue record for this book is available from the British Library

ISBN 0–141–31739-6

CONTENTS

Shhhhh!

At this very moment, millions of secret messages are whizzing around the world. They're being whispered into telephones, slipped through letter boxes and e-mailed from one computer to another. But what happens if those whispered conversations are overheard? What happens if those letters are opened by the wrong person or those computers fall into enemy hands?

The secrets are out – that's what!

Codes are a way of disguising messages. Once words have been coded, their meaning can be revealed only by someone who knows how to crack the code. So, even if a top-secret message is opened by the cleverest spy in the world – even one with a beige mac, red carnation, dark glasses and a copy of *The Times* – they won't be able to understand a single word.

Coded messages can look like a meaningless jumble of letters…

NVVG NV ZG MLLM*

They can look like an odd sequence of numbers...

13-5-5-20 13-5 1-20 14-15-15-14*

or just a single word...

fish.*

For thousands of years, cryptographers – people who study the art of secret writing – have invented masses of mind-boggling codes. Governments, spies and secret agents have used these codes to send and decode top-secret information that has won wars and even made a queen lose her head!

Codes can be split into two groups: codes and ciphers. A code uses a codeword to stand for a longer phrase. (For example, the code word 'fish' could really mean 'meet me at noon'.) A cipher uses letters, numbers or symbols to stand for other letters. But don't lose any sleep over the difference between codes and ciphers – in this book we'll just use the word 'code'.

Crack the Code is packed with highly confidential information. You'll find out how to code messages, how to decode them and where to hide them... The only special spy equipment you'll need to crack most of the codes is a pencil and a notebook.

So, are you ready to enter a world of mystery and intrigue? Have you got what it takes to unjumble the letters and find the secrets behind the strange symbols and mysterious messages? Grasp your pencil, take a deep breath, turn the page and... crack the codes!

PS You'll find all the answers to the Crack the Code *quiz questions in Chapter 11 (page 121).*

* See pages 14 (Number-cruncher) and 70 (ZYX) to find out how to decode these messages. The answers are also in the last chapter.

Chapter 1

SCRAMBLED CODES

The easiest way of coding a message is by simply scrambling the letters of the original words. You'll be astonished at how weird and wonderful words can look when they're all shook up…

Double Dutch

Make a secret word really difficult to read by writing the letters two by two! Leave plenty of space in between the pairs of letters and you will find that the original word is unrecognizable…

TULIPS

becomes

TU LI PS

If your message contains an odd number of letters, add an X after the last letter when you code it. This will fool any sneaky spies who may be hanging around!

MOUSE

becomes

MO US EX

7080583 **CRACK** 7 **THE** 3 **CODE** 46356252

Can you decode these Double Dutch messages?

CL OG SX

CA NA LS

WI ND MI LL

AM ST ER DA MX

374869670805834635625262888949

X-code

Secret notes often contain more than one word, so here's an eXtraordinarily eXcellent way to encode a marathon message...

Add an X after every single word before turning it into Double Dutch. For example:

TULIPS FROM AMSTERDAM

becomes

TULIPSX FROMX AMSTERDAMX

which becomes

TU LI PS XF RO MX AM

ST ER DA MX

This will make sure that the letters are well and truly muddled up – and will also make it easier for your code partner to read afterwards. You'll both know that when an X appears, you've probably reached the end of a word. (If you have an odd number of letters, add yet another X to the end of the coded message.)

Beware!
The letter X has been used to signal the end of a word because it's really rather a rare letter. However, in eXtremely eXtraordinary eXamples, if you remove the Xs to decode a message and find odd words such as 'e' and 'plode', don't despair. You may just have to add an eXtra X.

CRACK THE CODE

Can you figure out these X-coded messages?

TH EX NE TH ER LA ND SX

AX LI TT LE XM OU SE XW IT HX CL OG SX ON XX

ED AM XC HE ES EX IS XR EA LL YX TA ST YX

FL AT XC OU NT RI ES XA RE XG OO DX FO RX BI CY CL ES XX

Double-double Dutch

To make it even more difficult for the enemy to understand your Double Dutch code, swap the paired letters around! For example:

TULIPS

splits into pairs to become

TU LI PS

and then the pairs of letters are switched to become

UT IL SP

Again, if you have an odd number of letters, add a final X to complete the last pair.

CRACK THE CODE

7080583 ... 46356252

Can you unscramble these Double-double Dutch words?

ON SN NE ES

IG BB RE SI XH

AB DL RE AD HS

OG BB EL YD OG KO

374869670805834635625262888949

Sdrawkcab code

When they are written backwards, words can look like they're in a foreign language! For example:

BACKWARDS **becomes** SDRAWKCAB

Why not pretend that you're learning to speak a strange new language? You'll be able to communicate secretly, while astounding friends with your new 'language' skills!

Beware!

Avoid using palindromes in your message. These are words like noon that look exactly the same when they are written backwards, so they won't be coded at all. And you don't want to give the enemy any clues to help them decode your message, do you?

7080583 CRACK 7 THE 3 CODE 46356252

Can you make sense of these secret messages?

TNORF-OT-KCAB

OTNAREPSE

!UOY DNIHEB KOOL

ESROH EHT EROFEB TRAC EHT GNITTUP

37486967080583463562526288949

Anagrams

When the letters in a word are jumbled up to make a totally different word (or groups of words), this is called an anagram. For example:

The letters in the word

ANAGRAM

can be jumbled up to make these words

A RAG MAN

The same can be done with groups of words. CODES ARE EASY can be rearranged to read A SEA COSY DEER.

The word or words behind an anagram could leap out at you straight away, or you could puzzle over them for ages. Don't worry if you can't decode an anagram at once. Come back to it later – you might be surprised how quickly you spot the hidden message!

CRACK THE CODE

These anagrams are all hiding words that are linked with this book. Reading across, can you unscramble them?

COW RED DO	RED COAT CHECK
SAGE CRESS MEET	BUFFOON SKIP

Cracking facts!

Alexander Graham Bell (1847–1922) became famous throughout the world when he invented the telephone. But, after this resounding achievement, he didn't spend his time chattering on the phone to his best mates. Instead, he wrote articles for scientific magazines. However, he worried that he was being published because of who he was, not because of what he had written. To make sure that his articles were printed because they were good, the inventor used a pseudonym – a false name. He mixed up the letters of A. GRAHAM BELL to create the anagram H. A. LARGELAMB.

—•—•—•—•—•—•—

Galileo Galilei (1564–1642) was a famous scientist and astronomer. He often rearranged his discoveries into anagrams to confuse anyone cheeky enough to want to steal his ideas.

—•—•—•—•—•—•—

King Louis XIII of France (1601–43) loved anagrams so much that he employed Thomas Billon as the Royal Anagrammatist. It was Billon's full-time job to come up with witty anagrams of people's names.

—•—•—•—•—•—•—

Lewis Carroll (1832–98), the children's author, mathematician and incredibly clever inventor of codes, made a hobby of rearranging famous people's names to create anagrams that reflected the person's nature. The letters of Florence Nightingale, the famous Victorian nurse, were juggled to create the words 'Flit on, cheering angel'.

Chapter 2

SYMBOL CODES

Not all codes use letters. Symbols of all sorts – shapes, numbers, even dots and dashes – are all fantastic ways of making sure that a top-secret message stays top secret!

Number-cruncher code

Number the letters of the alphabet from 1 to 26 to turn messages into a puzzling stream of digits. If the enemy reads this code, it just won't add up!

Message	A	B	C	D	E	F	G
Code	1	2	3	4	5	6	7
Message	H	I	J	K	L	M	N
Code	8	9	10	11	12	13	14
Message	O	P	Q	R	S	T	U
Code	15	16	17	18	19	20	21
Message	V	W	X	Y	Z		
Code	22	23	24	25	26		

The letter A is coded as '1', B turns into '2' and so on. For example:

NUMBER becomes 14 21 13 2 5 18

Adding dashes in between the letters of the same word makes it easier to tell words apart and means that the coded message is easier to read. For example:

14-21-13-2-5-18

Why not give apostrophes, full stops, question marks and exclamation marks their own numbers? There are countless possibilities…

CRACK THE CODE

What do these strings of numbers really mean? Use the chart opposite to work out which letter each number stands for.

2-9-14-7-15

12-21-3-11-25 14-21-13-2-5-18

15-14-5 20-23-15, 2-21-3-11-12-5 13-25 19-8-15-5

15-14-5 20-23-15 20-8-18-5-5 6-15-21-18 6-9-22-5,
15-14-3-5 9 3-1-21-7-8-20 1 6-9-19-8 1-12-9-22-5

Criss-cross code

This may look like a weird game of noughts and crosses, but it's really the key to an ingenious code!

A	B	C
D	E	F
G	H	I

J•	K•	L•
M•	N•	O•
P•	Q•	R•

S••	T••	U••
V:	W••	X:
Y••	Z••	?••

To encode each letter, all you have to do is draw the shape that's around that letter.

For example, F becomes

Where there are one or two dots beside a code letter, draw these inside the shape too.

For example, T becomes ••

Invent your own mega-secret version of the criss-cross code. Just write the letters in a different order inside the criss-cross shapes. Then code each letter as usual!

CRACK THE CODE

Can you decode this short letter? Some of the words have been replaced by criss-cross code words.

Dear

I was

to to your

. However,

no has

. This is very and

totally . I am

very .

From (in)

PS I shall probably anyway!

Pigpen cipher

The criss-cross code is a different version of the pigpen cipher, which was invented hundreds of years ago. It was given its name because the shapes looked like pigpens. The original pigpen cipher arranged letters like this:

A	B	C
D	E	F
G	H	I

J•	K•	L•
M•	N•	O•
P•	Q•	R•

S, T, U, V

W•, X•, •Y, •Z

Text coded using the pigpen cipher looks similar to criss-cross code, apart from the letters S, T, U, V, W, X, Y and Z, which are very futuristic. For example, TUX becomes:

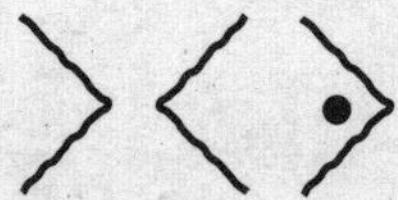

CRACK THE CODE

Decode this message to find out in which war the Pigpen cipher was first used.

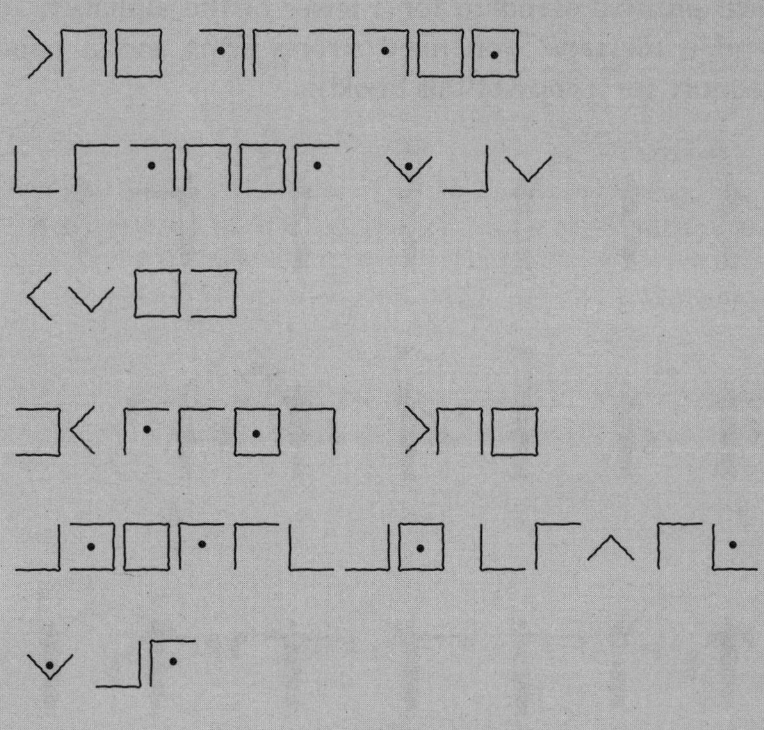

Semaphore code

Not all codes need to be written down. Semaphore, for example, is a system that uses two flags instead of a pen and paper. The flags are held in different positions, with each position standing for a letter of the alphabet. To send a message, you need strong arms and a good memory (or a copy of this book!).

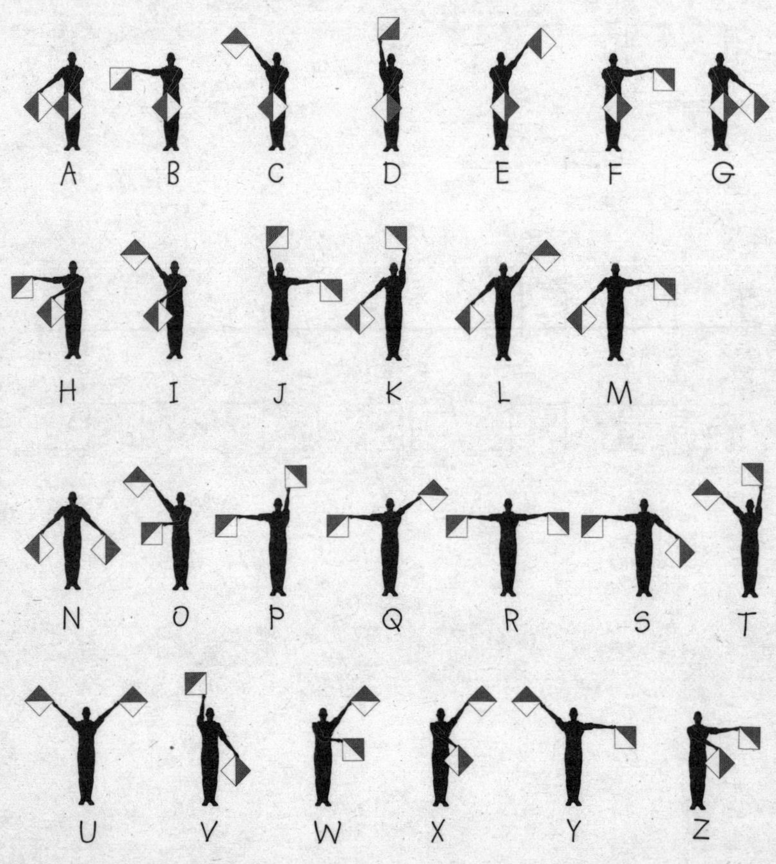

In semaphore, the word FLAG would look like this:

Semaphore is a type of communication rather than a code, but these days so few people know how it works that you can almost guarantee your messages won't be understood by anyone else…

CRACK THE CODE

Decode these messages or get your flags out and wave them to a friend across a large garden or playing field. (It's easier to recognize the signals from a distance.)

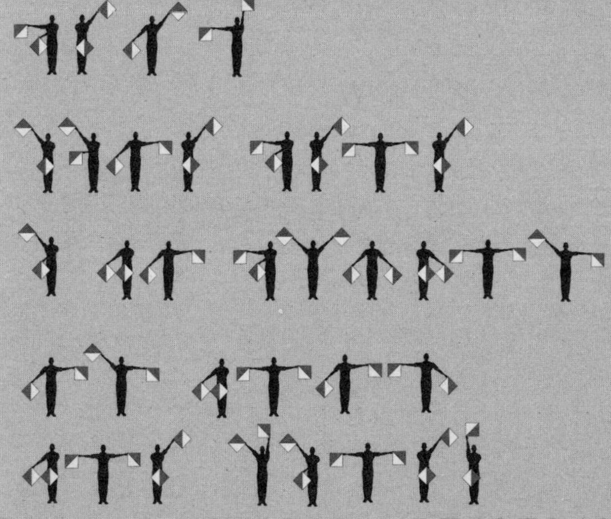

Morse code

Perhaps the most famous symbol code of all is Morse code. Here, different combinations of dots and dashes are used to stand for letters and punctuation.

When written down, Morse code looks like this:

A	·_	P	·__·
B	_···	Q	__·_
C	_·_·	R	·_·
D	_··	S	···
E	·	T	_
F	··_·	U	··_
G	__·	V	···_
H	····	W	·__
I	··	X	_··_
J	·___	Y	_·__
K	_·_	Z	__··
L	·_··	.	·_·_·_
M	__	?	··__··
N	_·	–	_····_
O	___	,	__··__

Although Morse code messages can be written down, the dots and dashes are usually sent as short and long beeps over a radio system. However, you could always speak Morse code aloud. Just substitute the word 'dit' for each dot and the word (can you guess what's coming…?) 'daa' for each dash – and remember to pause after each letter is completed.

7080583 CRACK 7 THE 3 CODE 46356252

Can you figure out the meaning of this Morse code message? A slash mark has been added after each word to make it easier to read. But beware – the real meaning might give you a nasty sinking feeling…

_•_• ___ __ • / •_ _ / ___ _• _•_• • / •_•_•_ /

•__ • / •••• •_ •••_ • / ••• _ •_• ••_ _•_• _•_ / •_ _• / •• _•_• • _••• • •_• __• / •_•_•_ /

•_• __ ••• / _ •• _ •_ _• •• _•_• /

37486967080583463562526288949

Cracking facts!

Code breakers use a technique called **frequency analysis** to crack substitution codes. (These codes work by swapping the letters of the alphabet with other letters, numbers or symbols.) In any language, some letters are used more often than others. In English, E, T and A are very common, and J, X and Z are very uncommon. The rest of the alphabet falls somewhere in between.

Code breakers use their knowledge of the frequency with which code letters or symbols appear. The code letter that appears most often in a secret message is likely to stand for E. Code breakers also look for commonly used groups of letters, so if the same three code letters appear lots of times, they may stand for common words such as 'the' or 'and'.

However, the best way to make a substitution code really hard to break is to keep messages short! The fewer the code letters, the fewer the clues for the code breaker...

—•—•—•—•—•—•—

Samuel F. B. Morse and Joseph Henry developed the electric telegraph system during the nineteenth century. Words could not be sent along telegraph wires – telephones were not invented until much later – only signals. Morse put his thinking cap on and invented **Morse code**. This allowed messages to be sent as a string of long and short signals, and then decoded at the other end of the telegraph line. But as anyone who knew Morse code could decode a message, people often scrambled up their messages before sending them!

Chapter 3

KEYPAD CODES

Mobile phones, computer keyboards and old-fashioned typewriters can be used to create 'data' that a rocket scientist would be proud of!

Telephone code

If you look at the buttons on any modern telephone, you'll see that there are letters as well as numbers printed on the buttons, like this:

Unless you've been living on the moon for the past ten years, you'll know that text messages are written on a mobile telephone by pressing each button a certain number of times. For example, the number 2 button is pressed once for an A, twice for a B and three times for the letter C.

This telephone code uses the text-message idea to turn words into a muddle of numbers. For example, when the number 4 button on a mobile phone is pressed twice, the letter H appears on its screen. So... the letter H would be written as 4(2). The first number refers to the button, the second to the number of times it's pressed. The word HELLO would turn into: 4(2) 3(2) 5(3) 5(3) 6(3).

Each time you see 0(1), leave a space and start decoding the next word.

CRACK THE CODE

Can you decode these messages?

Mobile shorthand

Avoid thumb-ache – send shorter text messages! There are loads of speedy ways of shortening words and phrases. (Some are well known and others are so complicated that even the person who invented them has forgotten what they mean.) If you and your friends make up your own, then no one will be able to decode them. Here are some common mobile shorthand phrases to inspire you…

4VR	for ever
ASAP	as soon as possible
BTW	by the way
DIY	do it yourself
LOL	lots of love
MYOB	mind your own business
NE	any
OIC	oh, I see
THX	thanks
TTFN	ta ta for now

CRACK THE CODE

Can you work out what these mobile-shorthand messages mean?

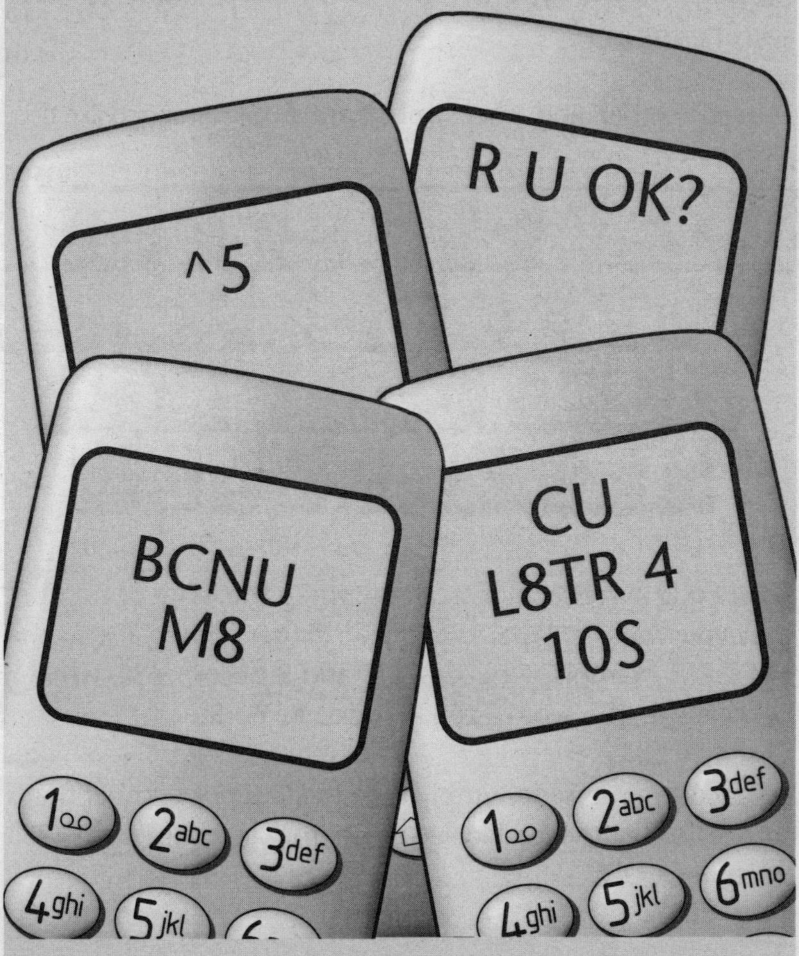

Keyboard code

With a computer keyboard, you have ready-made codes at your fingertips! You can use the keyboard code to encode a message as you type it – this is the perfect way to send secret e-mails.

Letters, numbers and other symbols are usually arranged like this:

To encode a message, instead of typing the letter or number that you want to type, move your fingers one place to the right. For example, F becomes G and B becomes N, while 7 becomes 8. The word TYPE is coded as YU[R.

To decode a message, simply type the letter or number that's to the left of the coded letter on the keyboard. So, VPFR becomes CODE.

CRACK THE CODE

Practise your keyboard skills with this coded encyclopedia entry...

WERTYU LRUNPSTFD

YJR ;RYYRTD PM UPIT VP,[IYRT LRUNPSTF STR OM YJR DS,R PTFRT SD YJPDR PM YJR GOTDY YU[RETOYRT = OMBRMYRF PBRT S JIMFTRF URSTD SHP/ OY OD VS;;RF S WERTYU LRUNPSTF NRVSIDR W. E. R. T. Y SMF U STR YJR GOTDY DOC ;RYYRTD PM YJR YP[TPE/

Up and over!

For more fingertip gymnastics, this time type the key that's above and slightly to the right. For example, Z becomes S, F becomes T and L becomes P. To decode a message, simply type the letter that's below and slightly left of the coded letter. So, F0R4 becomes CODE. (Numbers can't be coded – you'll have to spell them out.)

Keyboard hieroglyphics

You can use any symbols at all to stand for different letters. As long as you have 26 of them, you can code any message you like. There are plenty of curious characters on a computer keyboard – here are 26 of them to start you off:

Message	A	B	C	D	E	F	G
Code	«	@	#	¢	∞	§	¶
Message	**H**	**I**	**J**	**K**	**L**	**M**	**N**
Code	•	œ	∑	®	†	¥	ø
Message	**O**	**P**	**Q**	**R**	**S**	**T**	**U**
Code	π	ß	∂	ƒ	©	∆	Ω
Message	**V**	**W**	**X**	**Y**	**Z**		
Code	≈	ç	√	∫	µ		

This code will transform any message into ancient hieroglyphics. For example, TUTANKHAMUN'S TOMB looks like this:

∆ Ω ∆ « ø ® • « ¥ Ω ø ' ©

∆ π ¥ @

CRACK THE CODE

Can you work out what these mysterious messages mean?

« ¥Ω¥¥∫'© #Ωƒ©∞

∆•∞ ∞¶∫ß∆œ«ø ©ß•œø√

∆•∞ ≈«††∞∫ π§ ∆•∞ ®œø¶©

∆•∞ ¶ƒ∞«∆ ß∫ƒ«¥œ¢ π§ ¶œµ«

Cracking facts!

During the Second World War, it was vitally important for countries to keep their plans top secret. But information had to be sent somehow, so codes were used to disguise them. Here are two of the machines used.

— • — • — • — • — • — • —

The **Enigma machine** was a coding device used by the Nazis. It looked very like a typewriter, but when a letter was typed, a totally different letter would light up on the machine's display. This was the coded letter. Inside Enigma, there was a complex arrangement of wheels, plugs and reflectors that moved every time a letter was encoded. This meant that each time a letter was typed, it would be coded differently. AAA might be coded as KDC or FTS or LHO, and so on.

Messages coded using an Enigma machine could only be decoded using another Enigma machine – at least that's what its inventors thought. However, teams of Polish and then British code breakers proved them wrong. Years of painstaking work at Bletchley Park in Buckinghamshire, cracked the ever-changing Enigma codes over and over again, allowing the British to decode top-secret messages throughout the war.

— • — • — • — • — • — • —

Purple was the name for a Japanese code machine that used telephone switches to encode different letters. The code was cracked by US code breakers, allowing them to intercept important messages about planned attacks.

WIND OR RAIN DEAL CLOUD ONTO DARK EVEN SKIES WIND OR RAIN DEAL CLOUD ONTO DARK EVEN SKIES WIND OR RAIN DEAL CLOUD ONTO DARK EVEN SKIES WIND OR RAIN DEAL CLOUD ONTO DARK EVEN SKIES WIND OR RAIN DEAL CLOUD ONTO DARK EVEN SKIES WIND OR

Chapter 4
WORD CODES

Messages can be so well hidden in every day places – in poems, riddles, books, sentences and even recipes – that no one would suspect they were there!

WIND OR RAIN DEAL CLOUD ONTO DARK EVEN SKIES WIND OR RAIN DEAL CLOUD ONTO DARK EVEN SKIES WIND OR RAIN DEAL CLOUD ONTO DARK EVEN SKIES WIND OR RAIN DEAL CLOUD ONTO DARK EVEN SKIES WIND OR RAIN DEAL CLOUD ONTO DARK EVEN SKIES WIND OR

Acrostic code

Study the harmless-looking poem below. Would you believe that there's a secret word hidden among the letters? Can you spot it?

Crack this code.

Order the letters

Downwards. It's

Easy, when you know how!

The first letters of each line spell out the word CODE! This is an example of an acrostic – a poem or puzzle in which certain letters on each line spell out one or more words. Acrostics are ideal for short messages.

Why not write your own acrostics? Start with the letters of the secret message and then fill in the gaps with flowery or funny verse!

7080583 CRACK 7 THE 3 CODE 46356252

The names of two famous code-breaking machines are camouflaged among these strange commands. Can you spot them?

PLAY A TUNE UPON A TUBA

UNLOCK THE SECRET DOOR OF DOOM

RING THE BELL AND WAVE THE FLAG

PICK UP A PIZZA WITH PEPPERONI

LOOK INSIDE THE MYSTERIOUS CAVERN

ESCAPE FROM THE EVIL EYE

3748696708058346356252628889 49

Missing-word code

Coded words can be safely hidden among other words. This mysterious set of instructions is something you'd expect to find sewn inside the lining of a secret agent's suitcase. But what does it mean?

VISIT THE SHED BESIDE THE HOUSE TO DISCOVER THE SECRET MESSAGE. LOOK FOR A NUMBER OF RUSTY NAILS. NEARBY IS AN ENVELOPE. IT CONTAINS FIVE CLUES TO SOLVE.

Most of this message is utter nonsense! The real meaning is revealed when every fifth word is highlighted. Here's how:

VISIT THE SHED BESIDE **THE** HOUSE TO DISCOVER THE **SECRET** MESSAGE. LOOK FOR A **NUMBER** OF RUSTY NAILS. NEARBY **IS** AN ENVELOPE. IT CONTAINS **FIVE** CLUES TO SOLVE.

So... THE SECRET NUMBER IS FIVE. But anyone who just happens to find the note – when peeping inside the lining of the secret agent's suitcase – will be fooled!

CRACK THE CODE

Practise your spy skills by decoding these bizarre memos (Clue: they get harder as you go on!)

LOOK AT THE BIG CRACK ON THE WALL ABOVE THE BOOK SHELF. THE SECRET CODE IS HIDDEN INSIDE.

LOOK CAREFULLY – CAN YOU SEE THE TREE OVER THERE? YOU COULD CLIMB IT EASILY. AT THE TOP THERE ARE FIVE KITTENS MEWING LOUDLY.

CAN YOU QUICKLY GUESS WHAT MY RATHER BIZARRE AND VERY UNFASHIONABLE MIDDLE NAME IS? IS MY MIDDLE NAME ENGLEBERT, HUMPHREY OR QUENTIN, OR IS IT HORACE, SIEGFRIED, EBENEZER, ERSKINE, ALGERNON OR THEOBALD?

YOU MUST HAVE READ THE CLASSIC TALE TREASURE ISLAND! ROBERT LOUIS STEVENSON'S INCREDIBLY FAMOUS BOOK IS FILLED WITH ADVENTURE ON THE HIGH SEAS. IN TREASURE ISLAND, YOUNG STOWAWAY JIM HAWKINS MEETS THE SCARY PIRATE LONG JOHN SILVER. WITH A WOODEN LEG, AN ENORMOUS VOICE AND A HUGE CHEST, HE'S A REAL VILLAIN!

Book code

With so many words crammed between their covers, books provide the perfect material for countless secret messages. You can use any page of any book, as long as it contains the words that you want to include in your message. All you have to do is make a note of exactly where certain words appear in the text. The person decoding the message just needs a copy of the same book.

Here's an extract from a spooky book:

1 **Code words at midnight**
2 As the clock struck twelve, an icy breeze rushed through
3 the deserted house. The edges of old, crackling posters
4 curled away from the walls. Dusty books flew from shelves,
5 their pages madly flapping to and fro, as tattered
6 handwritten letters whirled into the air. In every room,
7 words rustled and danced in the cold wind.

8 Then, as if a switch had been flipped, the breeze
9 vanished and all was quiet. Now the floors were covered
10 with an alphabet carpet. A jumble of letters – large, small,
11 curly, typewritten, inky, coloured – lay on every surface.

12 But the letters all spelt out the same words: *The sly*
13 *brown fox jumped quickly over the lazy dog*. Was this a coded
14 message? What did it mean?

A coded message might look like this:

(line 1, word 1) (line 4, word 7)

If you search for these words in the story, you'll uncover the message: CODE BOOKS!

CRACK THE CODE

Read 'Code words at midnight' again. Can you work out what is special about the sentence 'The sly brown fox jumped quickly over the lazy dog'? Don't worry, the answer is hidden in the text. To find it, all you have to do is look for these words…

(line 9, word 3) (line 9, word 7) (line 6, word 2) (line 3, word 6) (line 2, word 2) (line 10, word 3)

Cookery code

This mouth-watering code is guaranteed to make you hungry! Read on to find out how a tasty message can be hidden in a list of ingredients...

Recipe

1 fancy cake decoration

3 mangoes or a large pineapple

3 pieces of chocolate

1 ice cube

3 cartons double cream

4 teaspoons bicarbonate of soda

This isn't a shopping list for a mango and chocolate pudding – it's a coded message! The number at the beginning of each ingredient tells you how many words to count. So, the first word of 'fancy cake decoration' is 'fancy' and the third word of 'mangoes or a large pineapple' is 'a'. Here's the list again, with all of the coded words highlighted:

Recipe

1 **fancy** cake decoration

3 mangoes or **a** large pineapple

3 pieces of **chocolate**

1 **ice** cube

3 cartons double **cream**

4 teaspoons bicarbonate of **soda**

The coded message is: Fancy a chocolate ice-cream soda?

CRACK THE CODE

Try your cookery code skills on this list of ingredients. Some words might be spelt in a slightly odd way, but just listen to how they sound and the message will make sense.

Recipe

Two things you'll need are an apron and a rolling pin.

For a successful recipe, have your oven nice and hot before you start cooking.

3 satsumas or a navel orange

2 cups really hot water

2 carrots (grate one of them)

2 teaspoons thyme

1 cooking apple

Bookworm code

Disguise your secret message as a list of books. If anyone sees the list, they'll just think that you're a keen reader!

For example, here are the titles of two books:

2. *The Secret Diary of Adrian Mole Aged 13 ¾* by Sue Townsend

5. *Artemis Fowl: The Eternity Code* by Eoin Colfer

To find the hidden meaning, look at the number before each title. The number 2 means that you should read the second word. The number five means that you should read the fifth word. So, the message is: SECRET CODE.

CRACK THE CODE

Can you crack these literary codes?

1. *My Mum's Going to Explode!* by Jeremy Strong

3. *The Dinosaur's Diary* by Julia Donaldson

3. *The Sky is Falling* by Kit Pearson

2. *Tom's Private War* by Robert Leeson

37486967080583463562526288949

1. *Time Stops for No Mouse* by Michael Hoeye

2. *The Four-Story Mistake* by Elizabeth Enright

4. *Midnight is a Place* by Joan Aiken

2. *Pirate School: The Birthday Bash* by Jeremy Strong

8. *Invasion of the Vampire Spiders* by Susan Gates

1. *I Managed a Monster* by Lesley Howarth

3. *Do You Want to be My Friend?* by Eric Carle

2345. *How to be a DJ* by Janet Hoggarth

1. *Come Back Gizmo* by Paul Jennings

4. *It Takes One to Know One* by Gervase Phinn

5. *Roll of Thunder, Hear My Cry* by Mildred D. Taylor

2. *Little House on the Prairie* by Laura Ingalls Wilder

2. *Pandemonium at School* by Jeremy Strong

8. *The Wonderful Story of Henry Sugar and Six More* by Roald Dahl

37486967080583463562526288949

Cracking facts!

Sherlock Holmes was a fictional detective with an amazing gift for solving crimes, mysteries... and codes. In the story *The Adventure of the Dancing Men* (1903), Sherlock Holmes is faced with a row of tiny pictures of dancing men frozen in various different positions.

The clever detective soon realizes that he is looking at a coded message: *'I am fairly familiar with all forms of secret writings... but I confess that this is entirely new to me. The object of those who invented the system has apparently been to conceal that these characters convey a message, and to give the idea that they are the mere random sketches of children. Having once recognized, however, that the symbols stood for letters, and having applied the rules which guide us in all forms of secret writings, the solution was easy enough.'*

Sherlock Holmes knows that E is the most common letter used in the English language, so he matches the dancing man that appears most frequently with this letter. Slowly he works his way through the alphabet until he has swapped all of the dancing men for letters. He solves the mystery because he knows how to crack the code.

Chapter 5

LETTER CODES

Single letters can be easily hidden inside words. The only way of finding them again is by knowing where to look…

1WES
T1OF
3FOR
D3HI
DE3S
ACK1
ON3
OLD2
LEDG
E4GL
ASS
1WES
T1OF
3FOR
D3HI
DE3S
ACK1
ON3
OLD2
LEDG
E4GL
ASS
1WES
T1OF
3FOR
D3HI
DE3S
ACK1
ON3
OLD2
LEDG
E4GL
ASS
1WES
T1OF
3FOR
D3HI

1WES
T1OF
3FOR
D3HI
DE3S
ACK1
ON3
OLD2
LEDG
E4GL
ASS
1WES
T1OF
3FOR
D3HI
DE3S
ACK1
ON3
OLD2
LEDG
E4GL
ASS
1WES
T1OF
3FOR
D3HI
DE3S
ACK1
ON3
OLD2
LEDG
E4GL
ASS
1WES
T1OF
3FOR
D3HI

Shopping-list code

This shopping list looks pretty normal. However, it conceals a coded message that describes what would happen if you ate everything on the list...

1 strawberry
1 turnip
2 tomatoes
4 salmon steaks
2 jalapeño peppers
6 garlic bulbs
4 fish fingers
3 pears
7 sticks celery
2 chocolate bars
11 syrup sponges

One coded letter is hidden in each shopping-list item. The number that appears before each scrummy item tells you where to find that letter. For example, '1 strawberry' means that you should write down the first letter of 'strawberry', which is S. '2 tomatoes' shows that the hidden letter is the second letter of 'tomatoes' – O. Here's the shopping list again, this time with all of the hidden letters revealed:

1 **s**trawberry
1 **t**urnip
2 t**o**matoes
4 sal**m**on steaks
2 j**a**lapeño peppers
6 garli**c** bulbs
4 fis**h** fingers
3 pe**a**rs
7 sticks **c**elery
2 c**h**ocolate bars
11 syrup spong**e**s

So, if you ate everything on this shopping list, you'd get a STOMACH ACHE!

CRACK THE CODE

7080583 4635625 2

Here are four more shopping lists for you to decode. The hidden words are linked with the items on the lists...

1 scotch egg	2 sausage rolls
9 sticks rhubarb	2 croissants
1 packet washing powder	5 cricket bats
3 cheesy triangles	2 television sets
7 toilet rolls	1 tub ice-cream
8 buffalo mozzarellas	

1 summery sandal	1 suede boot
10 tins polish	2 shoes
9 leather boots	4 insoles
6 trainers	4 flip-flops

2 ugly fruit	1 ripe apple
2 grapefruit	4 melons
6 oranges	4 avocados
4 limes	3 sweet potatoes
5 lemons	4 sharon fruit
4 mangoes	

1 towel	6 suitcases
11 tins insect repellent	9 pairs sunglasses
3 plane tickets	2 pens
1 velour tracksuit	6 playing cards
4 novels	6 sunhats
5 puzzle books	

37486967080583463562526288894 9

Telephone-number code

Why not hide secret messages in an address book? No one would ever think of looking for them there!

To non-experts, this might look like a totally normal list of telephone numbers. To experts – that's us – it looks like a cleverly hidden code word surrounded by some made-up names and numbers!

NAME	NUMBER
PAUL AND SUE	125887
THE HAIRDRESSER	483924
ROB AND SAM	298231
THE DENTIST	643206
KATIE AND SIMON	574992

To find the code word, you take the first number of each telephone number, then count the letters of each word. For example, the first number of '125887' is '1' and letter number 1 of 'PAUL AND SUE' is P. The fourth letter of 'THE HAIRDRESSER' is H, and so on. In this case, the code word is PHONE.

CRACK THE CODE

Take the phone off the hook and look carefully at these lists. Do the numbers ring any bells?

NAME	NUMBER
MILLY AND SAM	187961
GO-KART TRACK	205001
BARRIE	134714
PIPPA	202086
CARLISLE LIBRARY	719794
GREER	349523
POST OFFICE	183722
BOOKSHOP	628685
ROBERT	271118
SEREN	501369
ICE RINK	393133

NAME	NUMBER
WINDSURF CENTRE	420607
ROSALIE	239586
GOGERLY HOUSE	177050
JACK	267639
BOWLING ALLEY	670085
WOODY	400768
PUFFIN BOOKS	734365
THE COOPERS	577544
BULMAN RESTAURANT	633086
INGLEWOOD SCHOOL	584776

NAME	NUMBER
ADAM	267492
CATHERINE	747778
PAUL	277244
PIZZA PALACE	870253
JILL	388090
LINDA	267384
NANNA AND GRANDAD	726443
SWIMMING POOL	850383
MATT	376391
ROB CHAPMAN	246139
BEN NOËL	353024
CINEMA	460644

NAME	NUMBER
DIVA CAFÉ	300353
RAILWAY STATION	321477
DAN'S CARS	135933
TRAVEL AGENT	578572
JOSIE	237593
COMPUTER SUPPLIES	439582
CHEESE WORLD	256901
SKATE SHOP	819794
STAN	486606
BERT THE BARBER	783732

First-letter code

If you were sent the following sentence by a friend, would you think that they'd gone stark raving bonkers? Of course not! As an expert code breaker, you'd know that there was a secret message hidden within the words...

INSIDE NEW ICICLES THERE IS A LOVELY LONG ECLAIR THAT TASTES EXTRAORDINARILY (REALLY!) SCRUMPTIOUS.

The key to this code lies in the first letters of each word. Put them together and the code is cracked!

INSIDE **N**EW **I**CICLES **T**HERE **I**S **A** **L**OVELY **L**ONG **E**CLAIR **T**HAT **T**ASTES **E**XTRAORDINARILY (**R**EALLY!) **S**CRUMPTIOUS.

The letters spell: INITIAL LETTERS.

Messages encoded using this first-letter code don't have to make sense. Just use your imagination...

CRACK THE CODE

Can you spot the messages hidden on these envelopes?

Peacock Arms
Six Shirley Way
Oldham Road
Dunoon Magna
Alibutt University
V12 EHT

Hockey United
Ringcurran Rise
Yeoman

Sea Edge Enterprises
Yongleton-on-Udge
Attleborough Town
5UP

Codsall Orton Mews
Eleven Talbot-on-Thames Houses
Etterby Close
Inishbofin
Near Edward's Moor
Ailsham

Fifth-letter code

Get counting to reveal the word hidden in this slightly strange sentence! When put together, the fifth letters spell out a word...

A HAPPY CAMEL IN A NEW HAT AND MAC GIGGLES LOUDLY NOW.

The word is PENTAGON – a five-sided shape.

You can code messages where every third letter makes up a secret word. Or every fourth, sixth, seventh or twenty-seventh letter... Here's a tip – the higher the number, the easier it is to write the coded messages in the first place!

7080583 CRACK 7 THE 3 CODE 46356252

How do you shape up with these mysterious sentences?

COOL SHADE – QUICK, UNDER A CLEAR UMBRELLA!

A BUTTERED ROLL WITH TEA, LEMON AND A GREAT LIME WEDGE.

RED SHOES NEED MAXIMUM ART, PAGES, LOOKS – ANN.

BRAND-NEW BOOKS ADORE BEING ICY. STRANGE SHELF BESIDE DARK FRIDGE OF ORANGES.

3748696708058346356252626288949

Riddle code

Q: When is a riddle not a riddle? *A: When it's a code!*

Can you decode this ridiculous riddle?

My first is in prawn
My second is in bumblebee
My third is in maze
My fourth is in New Zealand
My fifth is in double
My sixth is in kettle

To crack this code, just follow each of the riddle's instructions. For example, the first letter of prawn is P, the second letter of bumblebee is U, the third letter of maze is Z, the fourth letter of New Zealand is Z, the fifth letter of double is I and the sixth letter of kettle is E. The hidden word is PUZZLE!

7080583 CRACK 7 THE 3 CODE 46356252

Can you work out the word hidden in this rhyming riddle?

My first is in rich
My second is in ditch
My third is in code
My fourth is in toad
My fifth is in myrtle
My sixth is in purple
What am I?

3748696708058346356252626288949

Cracking facts!

Samuel Pepys's diaries are famous for recording historic moments such as the Great Plague and the Great Fire of London. But did you know that Pepys (pronounced 'peeps') wrote in code? To make sure that no one discovered what he'd been up to, Pepys wrote in a little-known type of shorthand. He often recorded only the first syllable or letter of each word and, when recording details of his worst behaviour, Pepys used snippets of French, Spanish and even Latin. It took 122 years to decode!

— • — • — • — • — • — • —

Jane Eyre, *Wuthering Heights* and *The Tenant of Wildfell Hall* are among the classic novels written by the **Brontë sisters**. However, in the nineteenth century, books written by women were rare and the Brontës were worried that reviewers would highlight the fact that they were women and ignore the books themselves. So, they made up false names – Currer Bell (Charlotte Brontë), Ellis Bell (Emily Brontë) and Acton Bell (Anne Brontë).

— • — • — • — • — • — • —

Pilots and police use call signs to make sure that there are no misunderstandings in communication. Call signs are all very different words – they mean that the letter M (Mike) is never confused with N (November), S (Sierra) is never mixed up with F (Foxtrot)... You can use these call signs to make up your own secret messages.

A Alpha
B Bravo
C Charlie
D Delta
E Echo
F Foxtrot
G Golf
H Hotel
I India
J Juliet
K Kilo
M Mike
N November
O Oscar
P Papa
Q Quebec
R Romeo
S Sierra
T Tango
U Uniform
V Victor
W Whisky
X X-ray
Y Yankee
Z Zulu

Chapter 6

GRID CODES

If you can get hold of an exercise book filled with graph paper instead of ordinary lined paper, it will be much easier to code and decode the messages in this chapter.

Up-and-down code

Follow the instructions to turn a message into totally unrecognizable codswallop.

To code the message UP AND DOWN, first write the letters in a long line, like this (with no spaces):

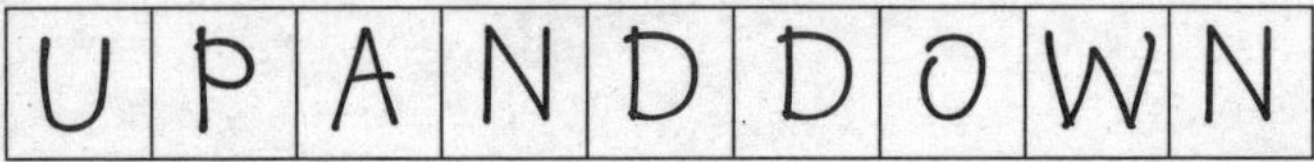

Then move every other letter down on to the row below.

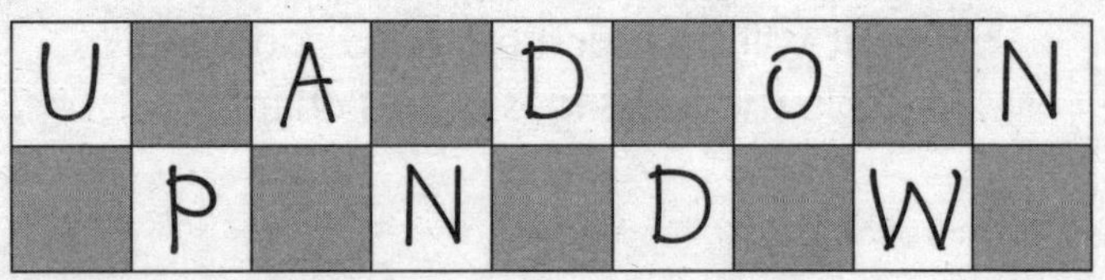

Next, write out the two rows of letters in the order they appear, going from left to right. Leave a space when you get to the end of the first line.

When you decode messages written in up-and-down code, the shaded square shows that you should start filling in the second row of boxes. Before you start, shade in two rows of boxes, so that you know where to write the coded letters:

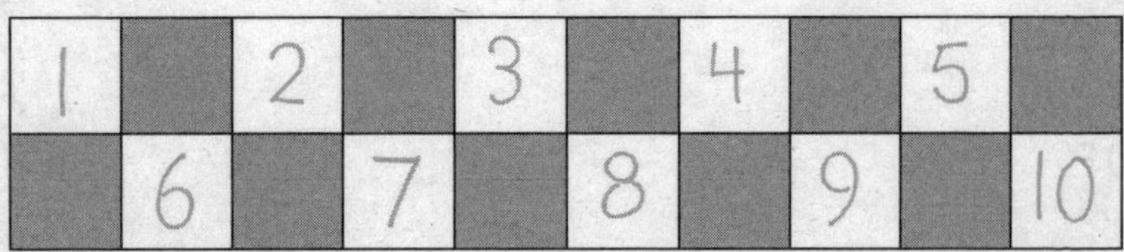

CRACK THE CODE

7080583 7 3 46356252

Remember to fill in the first and then the second row of boxes (starting a new row when you reach the shaded square). Then read up and down to decode the messages.

J	C	I	T	E	O		
	■	A	K	N	H	B	X

P	P	E	O	A	T	I	G	
	■	U	P	T	N	S	R	N

S	A	E	A	D	A	D	R		
	■	N	K	S	N	L	D	E	S

A	I	E	N	H	O	E	N	A	E		
	■	L	F	O	T	E	C	A	W	V	S

374869670805834635625262888949

Zigzag code

Here's how to make the up-and-down code even more difficult to decode. All you have to do is write the letters in a zigzag shape on three different lines. For example:

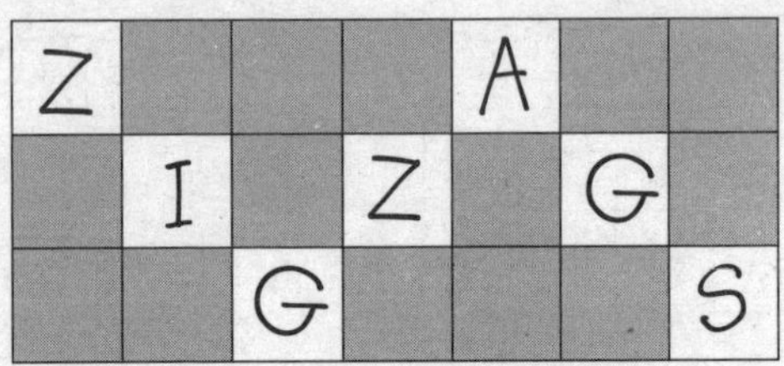

Next, write out the three rows of letters in the order they appear, going from left to right. Add a space when you reach the end of the first and second lines.

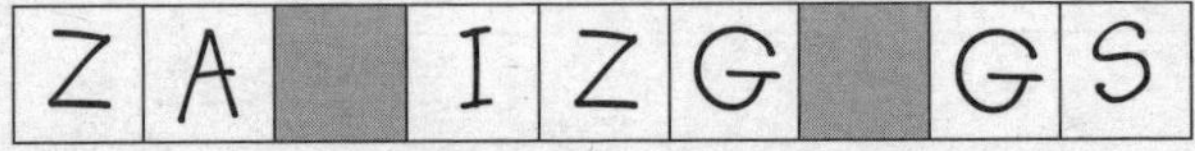

Before you start to decode, shade three rows of boxes like this.

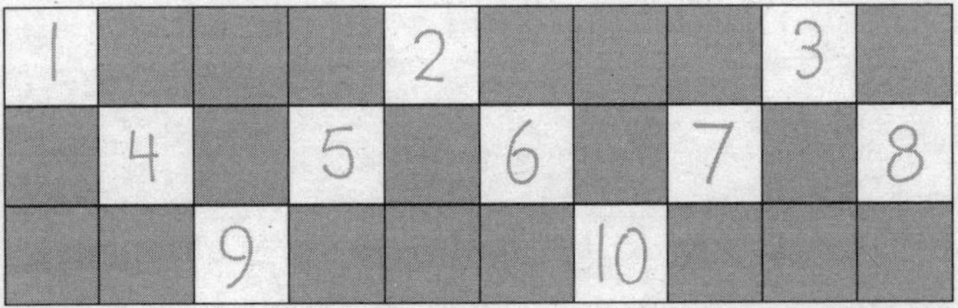

Then fill in the white squares, remembering to start a new row whenever you reach a shaded square in the original message.

CRACK THE CODE

Can you read these zigzag messages?

W	L	A		I	G	Y	O	D		G	R

C	K	A		R	O	E	P	T	
O	D	H							

T	T	D	N		W	S	S	N	T	R	S
	I	A	U								

U	A	A	O	T	S					
P	T	I	S	N	D	W	S	A	R	
S	R	D	N	I						

Twisted code

Here's another way to scramble a secret message! For this code, words are written into squares in a grid before being encoded in a really twisty way...

For example, the words TWISTED CODE can be written in a square grid, filling in the first line, then the second, third and fourth. Any leftover boxes at the end are filled with Xs.

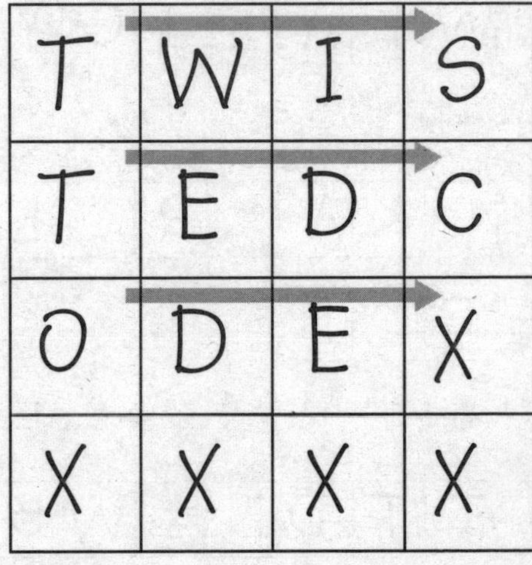

The message is coded by following a new twisty path through the grid and writing down the letters as you go. For example, you could travel down the first column, up the second, down the third and up the fourth.

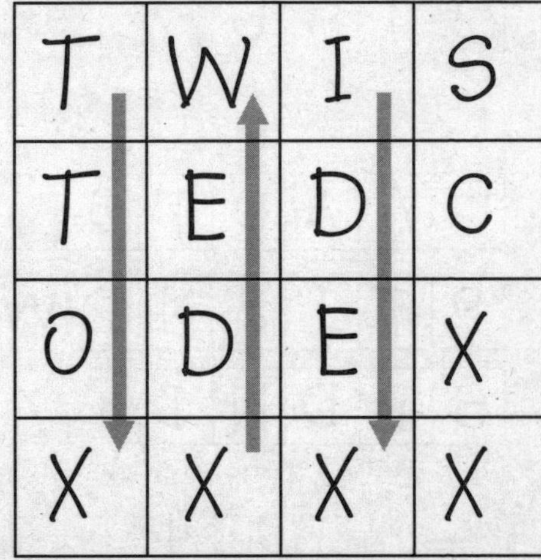

This gives the code: TTOXXDEWIDEXXXCS.

However, this many letters can be difficult to read (therefore difficult to decode), so group the letters together. If the grid is four squares wide, use groups of four letters. If it's five squares wide, use five-letter groups. As the grid here is four squares wide, TTOXXDEWIDEXXXCS becomes TTOX XDEW IDEX XXCS.

As long as your code partner knows that you coded the message starting in the top-left corner, working down and then up, they'll be able to decode the hidden words. Or alternatively invent your own secret path through the grid!

CRACK THE CODE

Try out your skills with these twisted codes. They are all written by starting in the top-left corner and working down, then up, down and up – as in the example.

MYOX XUGE RONX XDRR

HEER XLRE LSTX XEKT

TOAR NSRH EMTE DUHW

LSSA ITTE TWAN XGI '
(The apostrophe should be given its own square.)

Spiralling code

Instead of following a twisted path to encode your secret message, try spiralling inwards. Clockwise and anticlockwise spirals both work well – just make sure you tell your code partner which direction you followed to code the message. Otherwise, they'll be as dumbstruck as everyone else!

Clockwise spiral

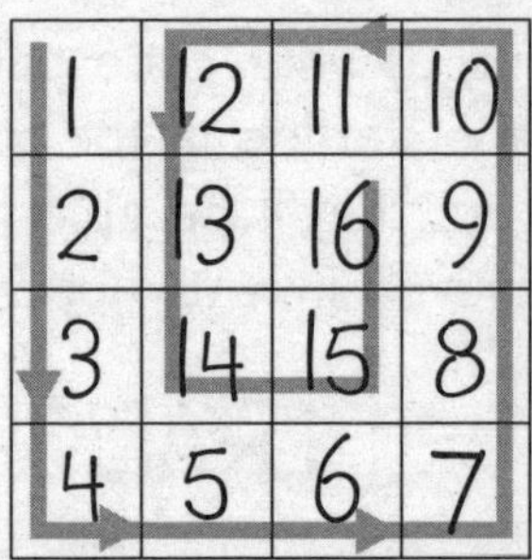

Anticlockwise spiral

The message SPIRALLING CODE is written into the grid in the same way as TWISTED CODE, adding X into the blank squares at the end.

S	P	I	R
A	L	L	I
N	G	C	O
D	E	X	X

Then, the message is coded in a clockwise or anti-clockwise spiral and split into groups.

Clockwise, it becomes SPIR IOXX EDNA LLCG

Anticlockwise it becomes SAND EXXO IRIP LGCL

The same message can look totally different depending on which way it is encoded!

CRACK THE CODE

Can you find the hidden meanings behind these spiralling code messages? The number of letters in each group shows how wide and how tall your grid should be.

WHI PLO ORL (Clockwise)

WRG IGI IHL (Anticlockwise)

SPIR TCXE SAAA LSRI (Clockwise)

ATORN SNSXX YAWGC ADOII IHTOM (Clockwise)

Odd-and-even code

There's nothing odd about this code! It's an extra-speedy way of making sure that no one can decode your secret communications.

Write your message into a row of squares on a piece of graph paper.

O	D	D	A	N	D	E	V	E	N	C	O	D	E

Directly beneath the letters, start writing the letters into every other square, starting with the first one. Stop when you have run out of letters to write beneath.

O	D	D	A	N	D	E	V	E	N	C	O	D	E
O		D		D		A		N		D		E	

Now go back to the beginning of the row and write the next seven letters of your message in the empty squares.

O	V	D	E	D	N	A	C	N	O	D	D	E	E

To decode the message, just write down the letters inside the odd-numbered squares (first, third, fifth...), followed by the letters inside the even-numbered squares (second, fourth, sixth...).

CRACK THE CODE

Can you decode these top-secret messages?

O	E	D	O	D	U	O	T	N

S	E	H	L	U	E	F	T	F	T

L	E	E	R	T	S	H

O	E	N	S	E	E	T	V	H	E	R	N

E	N	E	I	F	N	I	E	V

T	G	W	H	O	T	F	T	O	E	U	N	R	T	S

W	I	E	X	L	E	V	I	E

Cracking facts!

Secret messages have been hidden in the strangest of places. They've been sewn inside buttons, enclosed in false coins, swallowed (a stomach-churningly *bad* idea) and even thrown into wastepaper baskets for other spies to find. But the **Ancient Greeks** hid secret messages in a truly hair-raising place...

Around 400 BC, a Greek messenger carried a highly confidential memo right under the enemy's nose. It wasn't tucked in his pocket or hidden under his hat. Instead it was under his hair! Weeks earlier, the messenger's head had been shaved and the message was written on to his scalp. After his hair grew back, the messenger travelled to his destination, shaved his head and delivered the message!

—•—•—•—•—•—•—

This is quite a drastic way to hide a message. Here are some other ideas that are less likely to shock your mum...

Tuck a note...

- inside your sock
- inside the lining of a coat
- inside your belt

Hide a note...

- inside the pages of a book
- inside a sweet wrapper
- inside a CD or DVD case

Stick a note...

- to the underside of a rug
- to the back of a picture
- under a shelf
- under a table
- to the back of a drawer

Chapter 7
SWAP CODES

Here are five ways of changing letters and words into something completely different…

ZYX code

This code is as easy as ABC – or ZYX! All you have to do is write out the alphabet from left to right – then, beneath it, write the alphabet from right to left. The top row shows letters that haven't been coded and the bottom row shows what they turn into when they are coded.

Message	A	B	C	D	E	F	G
Code	Z	Y	X	W	V	U	T
Message	H	I	J	K	L	M	N
Code	S	R	Q	P	O	N	M
Message	O	P	Q	R	S	T	U
Code	L	K	J	I	H	G	F
Message	V	W	X	Y	Z		
Code	E	D	C	B	A		

When you code a message, look for each letter of your message on the top row and change it into the letter on the bottom row. For example:

ZYX CODE becomes ABC XLWV.

To decode the message, search for each letter on the bottom row and change it into the letter on the top row.

7080583 CRACK 7 THE 3 CODE 46356252

Practise your ZYX skills with these coded messages.

ZOKSZYVG

GDVMGB-HRC OVGGVIH

RG'H ZH VZHB ZH ZYX

WRXGRLMZIRVH ORHG DLIWH RM
ZOKSZYVGRXZO LIWVI

374869670805834635625262888949

Shift code

The shift code gets its name because the letters of the alphabet are shifted to make a coded message. Even when letters are shifted by just one, the new message can look totally different! Here, each letter is shifted one place to the left.

Message	A	B	C	D	E	F	G
Code	B	C	D	E	F	G	H
Message	H	I	J	K	L	M	N
Code	I	J	K	L	M	N	O
Message	O	P	Q	R	S	T	U
Code	P	Q	R	S	T	U	V
Message	V	W	X	Y	Z		
Code	W	X	Y	Z	A		

Using this code,

SHIFT CODE

becomes

TIJGU DPEF.

7080583 **CRACK THE CODE** 46356252

Shift these letters to find out the real meanings…

CVEHF VQ

NPWF TJEFXBZT

UBLF B TUFQ UP UIF
MFGU

VTF UIF OFYU MFUUFS JO
UIF BMQIBCFU

37486967080583463562526288949

Multiple-shift code

Of course, you can shift letters any number of places to code them. Here's a grid that will allow you to use any of the twenty-five shift codes.

Message	A	B	C	D	E	F	G	H	I	J	K	L	M	N	O	P	Q	R	S	T	U	V	W	X	Y	Z
1-shift	B	C	D	E	F	G	H	I	J	K	L	M	N	O	P	Q	R	S	T	U	V	W	X	Y	Z	A
2-shift	C	D	E	F	G	H	I	J	K	L	M	N	O	P	Q	R	S	T	U	V	W	X	Y	Z	A	B
3-shift	D	E	F	G	H	I	J	K	L	M	N	O	P	Q	R	S	T	U	V	W	X	Y	Z	A	B	C
4-shift	E	F	G	H	I	J	K	L	M	N	O	P	Q	R	S	T	U	V	W	X	Y	Z	A	B	C	D
5-shift	F	G	H	I	J	K	L	M	N	O	P	Q	R	S	T	U	V	W	X	Y	Z	A	B	C	D	E
6-shift	G	H	I	J	K	L	M	N	O	P	Q	R	S	T	U	V	W	X	Y	Z	A	B	C	D	E	F
7-shift	H	I	J	K	L	M	N	O	P	Q	R	S	T	U	V	W	X	Y	Z	A	B	C	D	E	F	G
8-shift	I	J	K	L	M	N	O	P	Q	R	S	T	U	V	W	X	Y	Z	A	B	C	D	E	F	G	H
9-shift	J	K	L	M	N	O	P	Q	R	S	T	U	V	W	X	Y	Z	A	B	C	D	E	F	G	H	I
10-shift	K	L	M	N	O	P	Q	R	S	T	U	V	W	X	Y	Z	A	B	C	D	E	F	G	H	I	J
11-shift	L	M	N	O	P	Q	R	S	T	U	V	W	X	Y	Z	A	B	C	D	E	F	G	H	I	J	K
12-shift	M	N	O	P	Q	R	S	T	U	V	W	X	Y	Z	A	B	C	D	E	F	G	H	I	J	K	L
13-shift	N	O	P	Q	R	S	T	U	V	W	X	Y	Z	A	B	C	D	E	F	G	H	I	J	K	L	M
14-shift	O	P	Q	R	S	T	U	V	W	X	Y	Z	A	B	C	D	E	F	G	H	I	J	K	L	M	N
15-shift	P	Q	R	S	T	U	V	W	X	Y	Z	A	B	C	D	E	F	G	H	I	J	K	L	M	N	O
16-shift	Q	R	S	T	U	V	W	X	Y	Z	A	B	C	D	E	F	G	H	I	J	K	L	M	N	O	P
17-shift	R	S	T	U	V	W	X	Y	Z	A	B	C	D	E	F	G	H	I	J	K	L	M	N	O	P	Q
18-shift	S	T	U	V	W	X	Y	Z	A	B	C	D	E	F	G	H	I	J	K	L	M	N	O	P	Q	R
19-shift	T	U	V	W	X	Y	Z	A	B	C	D	E	F	G	H	I	J	K	L	M	N	O	P	Q	R	S
20-shift	U	V	W	X	Y	Z	A	B	C	D	E	F	G	H	I	J	K	L	M	N	O	P	Q	R	S	T
21-shift	V	W	X	Y	Z	A	B	C	D	E	F	G	H	I	J	K	L	M	N	O	P	Q	R	S	T	U
22-shift	W	X	Y	Z	A	B	C	D	E	F	G	H	I	J	K	L	M	N	O	P	Q	R	S	T	U	V
23-shift	X	Y	Z	A	B	C	D	E	F	G	H	I	J	K	L	M	N	O	P	Q	R	S	T	U	V	W
24-shift	Y	Z	A	B	C	D	E	F	G	H	I	J	K	L	M	N	O	P	Q	R	S	T	U	V	W	X
25-shift	Z	A	B	C	D	E	F	G	H	I	J	K	L	M	N	O	P	Q	R	S	T	U	V	W	X	Y

When you're encoding a message, just remember to let your code partner know the number of the shift you are using. You could put the number at the beginning of the message – no one else will know what the numbers mean!

For example, when SHIFT CODE is encoded using the 5-shift row of the grid, it becomes (5) XMNKY HTIJ. The number 5 tells the decoder to look for the letters on the fifth row of the grid.

7080583 CRACK 7 THE 3 CODE 46356252

Try these coded messages! They are all names of people who have invented different codes – you can find out about them elsewhere in this book…

(3) MXOLXV FDHVDU

(10) VOGSC MKBBYVV

(25) AKZHRD CD UHFMDQD

(8) AQZ IZBPCZ KWVIV LWGTM

3748696708058346356252628889 49

Random-letter code

You don't have to stick to the shift codes mentioned in this chapter. Why not make up your own code? Just pop the letters of the alphabet in any box, making sure that you use each letter once and only once!

Message	A	B	C	D	E	F	G
Code	F	W	O	I	H	J	Q
Message	H	I	J	K	L	M	N
Code	A	C	P	Z	X	G	L
Message	O	P	Q	R	S	T	U
Code	U	B	K	Y	V	R	D
Message	V	W	X	Y	Z		
Code	T	M	N	S	E		

Using this particular code,

RANDOM-LETTER CODE

becomes

YFLIUG-XHRRHY OUIH.

Make sure the person you are writing to also has a copy of your grid.

7080583 CRACK 7 THE 3 CODE 46356252

Using the same key, work out who this postcard is for and what it says, then follow the instructions.

OULQYFRDXFRCULV!
SUD'TH OYFOZHI RACV
OUIH! LUM RDYL RAH
BFQH RU XHFYL GUYH
OUUX MFSV UJ
MYCRCLQ VHOYHR
GHVVFQHV...

F OUIHWYHFZHY
VHOYHR VRYHHR
ACIIHL RUML

3748696708058346356252628889 49

Cracking facts!

The **Caesar cipher** is a type of shift code where each letter is shifted three places to the right which is exactly the same as the third row of the multiple-shift grid on pages 74-5. The code was named after the Roman general Julius Caesar (*c*.100–44 BC) who often coded messages in this way.

— • — • — • — • — • — • —

The multiple-shift grid is also known as the **Vignère square** named after a French politician, Blaise de Vignère, who invented it in the sixteenth century. However, Vignère had a much more complicated way of using it. Instead of coding a message using just one row of the grid, he would code each letter using a different row. This meant that the code was very difficult to break. Some people said that it was unbreakable but, **Charles Babbage**, a brilliant mathematician who had the idea for the first computer, set about proving them wrong. He eventually achieved his aim, breaking the code an amazing two centuries after it was invented.

To encode words using an easier version of the Vignère square, first choose two numbers between 1 and 25, for example, 1 and 25. Above your message write 1 and 25 alternately, like this:

1	25	1	25	1	25	1		25	1	25	1	25	1	25
C	H	A	R	L	E	S		B	A	B	B	A	G	E

To code the first letter, look along row 1 of the grid (page 74) for the letter under C. To code the second letter, look along row 25 for the letter under H. When the entire message has been coded, it turns into DGBQMDT ABACZHD. With practice, you too will be able to write coded messages that will take 200 years to crack!

Chapter 8

GADGET CODES

There are lots of ingenious gadgets for coding and decoding messages. This chapter shows you how to make and use them.

Toilet-roll code

You might think that the only thing that should be wrapped round a toilet-roll tube is toilet paper, but you'd be wrong. You can wrap coded messages round too!

What you need

Scissors
Sticky tape
2 cardboard toilet-roll tubes
(make sure they are the same size)
Pen or pencil
Sheet of paper

What you do

1. Cut two long strips of paper, about 2 centimetres wide and 30 centimetres long, from the sheet of paper. Stick the ends of these strips together to make a narrow but extra-long piece of paper.

2. Stick one end of the paper strip to the edge of the toilet-roll tube. Then wind the paper round and round and round and stick the other end of the strip to the tube.

(NB The paper should be stuck on an angle, so that it can be wound round without puckering.)

3. Now write your message across the strips of paper, like this:

4. Unwind the paper and fill in the gaps with random letters and numbers for extra secrecy. It then looks like a list of nonsense.

5. The only way to read the coded message is to wrap it round a toilet-roll tube once more…

If you don't have a toilet-roll tube handy, you could wrap your messages around a kitchen-roll tube, a rolling pin or even a fat marker pen. Just make sure your code partner knows what you have used.

Why not hide your message inside the tube that you used to code it? A rolled-up strip of paper can easily be slotted inside the cardboard tube and will then unroll until it fits the space. Who would ever think of looking for a message here?

Grille code

Look at these letters. Do they mean anything at all?

Z	S	E	J	E
Y	O	P	U	Q
L	A	T	R	S
K	L	I	X	N
P	P	A	M	T

Yes! There's a secret message hidden among the letters! But you need a special code gadget to find out what that message is…

A grille is a square of cardboard with holes cut into it. When it's placed over the jumble of letters, the hidden message can be read through the holes!

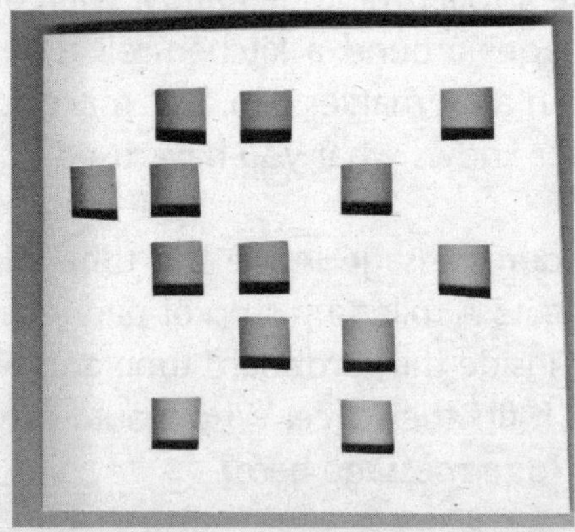

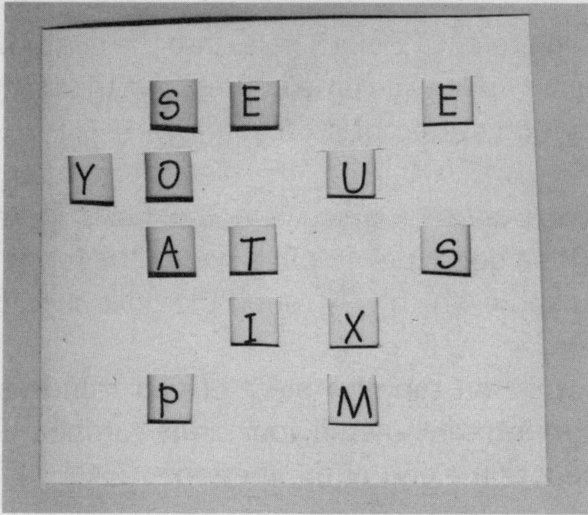

By reading along the rows from left to right, the message is revealed SEE YOU AT SIX PM. So here's how to do it…

What you need

Cardboard
Ruler
Pen or pencil
Scissors or craft knife

What you do

1. Cut out a cardboard square measuring about 13 centimetres by 13 centimetres.

2. Draw a grid – five squares by five squares – as a guide for where the grille's holes should go.

3. Ask an adult to cut 12 or 13 holes into the cardboard grille for you. A craft knife will come in useful for this. (This part is very tricky – don't attempt it on your own!)

4. Now make another grille with the holes in the same positions. (It's a good idea to put a sign in the top-left corner so that you know which way round the grille should go.)

5. Lay the grille on top of a piece of paper and write your message through the holes in your crafty cardboard gadget. Use X to denote the end of the message.

6. Remove the grille and fill the blank spaces with random letters to fool the enemy!

7. Give the second grille to your code partner so they can read your messages.

Flip it or spin it!
You can make a code even more difficult to break by flipping the grille over before writing your message in the holes. Just make sure your code partner knows which way up they should use the grille in order to decode the message.

Grilles can even be spun round to different positions. Write a letter in each corner. When you write your message, remember which letter was in the top-left-hand corner. You can whisper this letter to your code partner when passing on the message, so they know how to decode it!

CRACK THE CODE

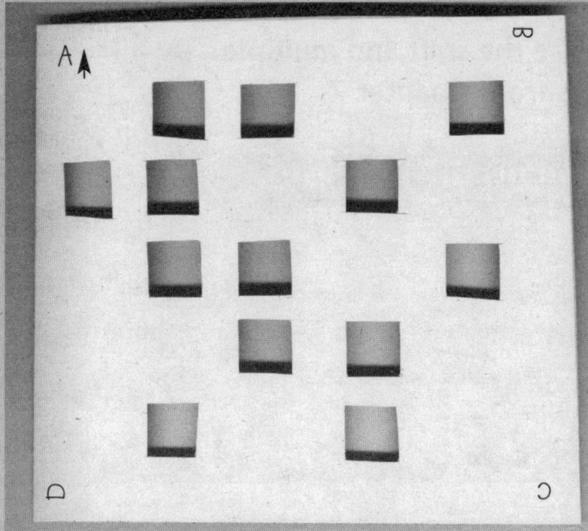

Using the grille above, find out which French cardinal used this gadget to code his secret messages:

S R I L C

H E E L D

P I E M U

J N X L O

A B E X R

Code wheel

This handy device makes it even easier to use the shift and multiple-shift codes from Chapter 7.

What you need

Cup
Saucer
Cardboard
Scissors
Split drawing pin
Pen or pencil

What you do

1. Place the cup and saucer face down on to the cardboard and draw around each of them.

2. Carefully cut out the two circles.

3. Stick the split pin through the centre of the smaller card circle and then through the centre of the larger card circle. Bend the ends of the pin outwards so that the circles are fixed together.

4. Write the letters of the alphabet around the smaller circle and then the larger circle, so they are lined up.

If you find it easier, trace these circles to make your code wheel.

That's it! Now you're ready to code your messages!

If you want to use the shift code (page 72), move the smaller code wheel one space to the left so that Z (on the big wheel) lines up with A on the small wheel. To code a message, find the letter on the big wheel and write down the matching letter on the smaller wheel. So, A becomes B and B becomes C, etc. To decode a message, look for the letter on the smaller wheel and write down its corresponding letter on the larger wheel. (It might help to write 'CODE' on the smaller wheel and 'MESSAGE' on the larger one, so you remember which is which.)

Now you can go back to the coded messages on page 73 and work out their meanings, this time using the code wheel!

If you want to use the multiple-shift code (page 74), move the smaller code wheel the same number of places to the left as the number of the shift code you want to use! So, for line 8 of the code grid, move the smaller wheel eight spaces to the left.

CRACK THE CODE

Spin your wheel to work out these secret codes.

(1) TQJOOJOH XIFFM

(7) YVBUK HUK YVBUK

(12) ITQQXK RMN

(25) FNHMF QNTMC HM BHQBKDR

Paperclip code

Even the most everyday objects can be used to code and decode messages. No one will ever guess that a small paperclip is actually a high-tech code gadget...

What you need

Ruler
Pen or pencil
Paperclip
Piece of paper

What you do

1. Draw a margin on the left-hand side of the piece of paper. This is your starting point.

2. Place your paperclip beside the starting point. Then write the first letter of your coded message inside the small opening of the paperclip, like this:

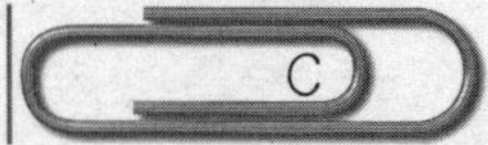

3. Move the paperclip along to the right until the letter is just inside the paperclip's larger opening. Now you can write the second letter of your message.

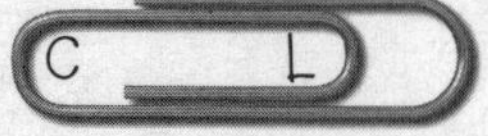

4. In this way, write your entire message, moving the paperclip one space to the right for each letter. (When you

reach the right-hand edge of the page, move down a line, using the same vertical line as a starting point.)

5. At the end of each word there should be a special symbol known only to you and your code partner. This is also the beginning of the next word. In this example, the symbol is *.

| C L I P *

6. Now, all you have to do is fill in the gaps with extra letters and numbers!

| TRACKS LIKE IN A PAW P*INT

Don't worry if the extra letters don't mean anything – any nonsense will do.

CRACK THE CODE

Using a paperclip the same size as above, work out the hidden meaning inside this stream of nonsense.

A CODE TOOWN * FRONT STOP LET
EVEN*BALL THE SHOT SET*SENT
CLOTHALPEN A*CARP STAR POP
CLOSE BLUR BACKGIRL AND IT'S GAP
YEAR*STRIFS MARVELLOUSLOUD*
NOISIESTIN THE TOWN OR IT * GAVE
IT INSIDE WEMBLEY YET*WICH
HAVE A MANGO DRY SATS *MA!

Ruler code

You don't need glue, pipe cleaners or sticky-back plastic to make this code gizmo – you've probably already got one inside your school bag. A ruler!

What you need

Ruler
Pen or pencil
Piece of paper

What you do

1. Draw a margin down the left-hand side of a piece of paper.

2. Hold your ruler across the page, lining up its left edge with the line you've drawn. Then write each letter of your message above a centimetre mark, like this:

3. Put an * after the last word of your message so that the decoder knows when to stop decoding.

4. Now fill in the gaps with other letters, numbers and

symbols. You could even write different words in between.

|SJRIPU25LADEAWRKB*LO

For added mystery, you could write each letter of your message above the 2cm, 4cm, 6cm (and so on) marks on your ruler. If you're a real whiz at times-tables, try using multiples of three (3cm, 6cm, 9cm, 12cm...) or four (4cm, 8cm, 12cm, 16cm). You'll be amazed at how strange your message looks when the new letters have been added, and no one will ever work out what they really mean...

7080583 CRACK THE CODE 46356252

With your ruler at the ready, measure these codes. The letters have been written above each centimetre mark.

|ARCSNEEDNEWT TI N MOSE ZATOORE NE*

|2OO PAN 73E L LTARWOOO DJTRA HEARSEE
XOEORFZ OLL UOOR MFNOIKEVY YE*

|YOAUCLOUOLDNEVGENSWRTIT REAANOI
THGERHMETSSMAGEIN SBESTWAEEGNLE*

|THMISEIS AONSEOUSFRHAEKEFSPOEA R
REM'S EAYASTSAEUYA RREEPE*

3748696708058346356252626288894 9

Cracking facts!

The toilet-roll code in this chapter uses an up-to-date version of a code gadget first used by the Spartans – ancient Greeks famed for their strength and fitness. The ***scytale*** was a rounded wooden stick around which was wrapped a long, thin piece of leather. A message was then written across the strips of leather and, when this was unwound, the message was totally scrambled. If anyone wanted to read this message, they had to wrap the leather around a *scytale* that was exactly the same size.

—•—•—•—•—•—•—

In 1777, during the **American Revolution**, British soldiers sent coded messages to each other. In one letter, Sir Henry Clinton, a British general, placed a grille with a large hole the shape of a butternut squash over a piece of paper and wrote his message inside. He then removed the grille and added other words around his message that cleverly reversed the meaning of the original letter!

—•—•—•—•—•—•—

The **code wheel** was invented by Italian architect Leon Battista Alberti in the fifteenth century. The original code wheel was more hard-wearing than the one shown on page 88. Instead of cardboard, Alberti used sheets of copper to make two discs, which he fitted together with a pin. However, both Alberti's wheel and the cardboard code wheel do exactly the same job!

Chapter 9

CUNNING CODES

Just when you thought there couldn't possibly be any more codes, here are five more to confuse and confound nosy parkers!

Mirror code

Messages written in this code can only be read using a mirror. And it's easier than you might think to do mirror writing…

What you need

Pen or pencil	Paper
Tracing paper or greaseproof paper	Mirror

What you do

1. Write your message on to the tracing paper.

2. When you turn the tracing paper over, your writing will be transformed into mirror writing!

3. Now all you have to do is copy the mirror message on to a normal piece of paper.

4. To read mirror writing, hold a small mirror to the right or left of the message, or simply hold the message in front of a larger mirror.

5. Why not encode your messages using another code in this book and then transform them into mirror writing? No one will be able to crack them!

7080583 CRACK 7 THE 3 CODE 46356252

Grab your mirror and work out what these messages really mean!

MIRROR MIRROR ON THE WALL

Through the Looking-glass

The following messages have been coded using the ZYX code on page 70 and then turned into mirror writing. So, first reflect them and then decode them!

OVLMZIWL WZ ERMXR

MZIXRHEH UVOO RM OLEV
DRGS SRH LDM IVUOVXGRLM

3748696708058346356252626288949

See-through code

Here's another code that uses tracing paper and your favourite book to disguise a message.

What you need

Book
Tracing paper or greaseproof paper
A pencil (not too sharp)

What you do

1. Find a page in a book. (Remember to keep the name of the book and the number of the page a secret between you and your code partner!)

Code words at midnight

As the clock struck twelve, an icy breeze rushed through the deserted house. The edges of old, crackling posters curled away from the walls. Dusty books flew from shelves, their pages madly flapping to and fro, as tattered handwritten letters whirled into the air. In every room, words rustled and danced in the cold wind.

2. Place the tracing paper over the page and draw circles around letters, groups of letters or words to spell out your message.

3. Put '1' beside the circle to be read first and '2' beside the next, until all the circles are numbered.

4. Trace over the first and last words that appear on the page.

5. When the tracing paper is removed, the code will look something like this – totally meaningless!

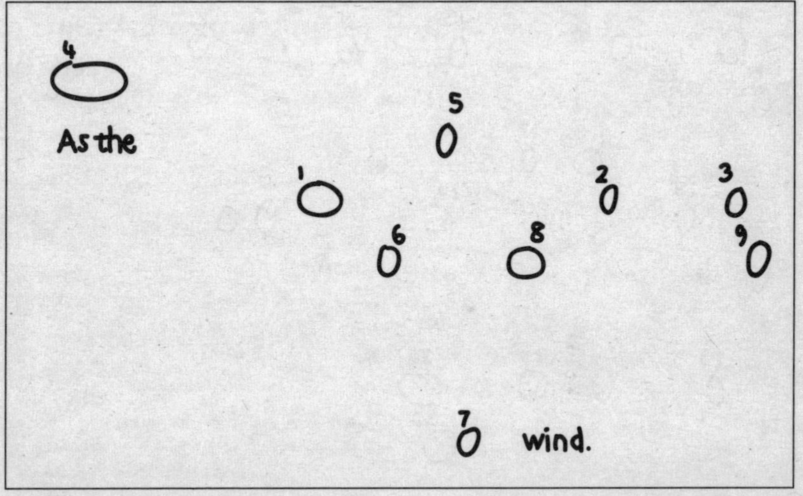

6. To read the message, place the tracing paper over the correct page, lining up the first and last words with the traced letters. Now read the numbered letters in order.

CRACK THE CODE

Trace this pattern on to a piece of tracing paper, then place it over the story on the next page. Can you find the hidden message?

Code

mean...?

Code words at midnight

As the clock struck twelve, an icy breeze rushed through the deserted house. The edges of old, crackling posters curled away from the walls. Dusty books flew from shelves, their pages madly flapping to and fro, as tattered handwritten letters whirled into the air. In every room, words rustled and danced in the cold wind.

Then, as if a switch had been flipped, the breeze vanished and all was quiet. Now, the floors were covered with an alphabet carpet. A jumble of letters – large, small, curly, typewritten, inky, coloured – lay on every surface.

But the letters all spelt out the same words: *The sly brown fox jumped quickly over the lazy dog*. Was this a coded message? What did it mean...?

Crossword code

Some crosswords can be fiendishly difficult, but you don't have to solve them. There's a really easy way of using them to code messages instead.

Look in old newspapers until you find an empty crossword. (Warning – make sure that the owner of the newspaper never wants to do the crossword. There's nothing worse than cross words from a cross crossword addict.) You'll notice that there are tiny numbers in some of the squares. Write your message into these squares, starting with 1, then 2, then 3, etc. Here, the message is CODEWORDS.

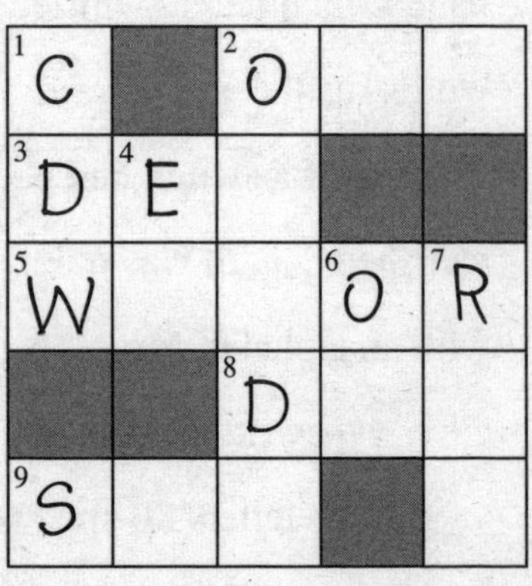

1 C	■	2 O	D	D
3 D	4 E	P	■	■
5 W	E	E	6 O	7 R
■	■	8 D	A	D
9 S	O	S	■	S

Now fill in the rest of the crossword with any words or letters that you can think of – the weirder the better!

Decoding the message is simple. All you have to do is look for the numbered squares and read them in the right order.

CRACK THE CODE

Find the secret words hidden in these crosswords...

1 C	2 R	3 O		
4 S	O	N	5 S	
6 W	A	L	I	7 O
	8 R	I	L	U
		9 D	O	T

1 S	N	2 O			3 L
L		4 V	O	K	E
E		E			T
D			5 E		T
6 I	O	N	S		E
T			7 T	O	R

1 C	R	2 O	P	I	3 N
L		D			E
4 U	5 N	A		6 D	E
7 R	A		8 U	O	D
I			N		L
9 M	O	O	N	B	E

1 C	2 R	3 A		4 C	5 K
6 T	O	R	7 H		E
8 E	O	D	O	9 C	E
10 O	F	O	L	O	P
L		11 D	O	L	M
12 E	M		13 S	D	Y

Origami code

Origami is the Japanese art of folding paper into imaginative shapes. It's also the perfect way to disguise secret words. Here's how to send a message that looks to the non-expert like a normal folded-up note.

Fold a blank piece of paper in half, then in half again, pressing firmly as you do so. Open it up to reveal a still blank, but very creased piece of paper. Now write your message down and then along the creases, like this:

DEAR MARTIN
HEY! GREAT IDEA!
HOW ABOUT ME AND YOU
GET TOGETHER
TO DO HOMEWORK AFTER
SCHOOL TONIGHT
WE'VE GOT
ENGLISH MATHS
PHYSICS FRENCH
ART
SPANISH GEOGRAPHY
HISTORY

Then fill up the spaces with real or nonsense words – or both!

You can fold a piece of paper any way you like – horizontally, vertically, even diagonally. Add Xs to the end of your message if you still have creases to fill.

CRACK THE CODE

Look at these creased notes carefully. What can you see?

ELEPHANTS NEED
MILK AND BISCUITS
PLENTY OF RUNNING
AROUND OR
A GA TE
TO E SCAPE
THROUGH AT NIGHT
TI GERS CANTER
N EARBY A YARD
IN
THE VILLAGE MAR-
KET PLACE, THEN EAT

APRIL FOOL ATE TRIFLE
AND ORANGES AFTER
FALLING TOWARDS
ANDOVER OR DEVON
KETCHUP CHIPS
AND MAKING PIE AND ROAST
PARSNIPS. EATING LEAN
PORK CHOPS WAS TINGLY

ABD CFGDFED RDDFE G
QRSRTUABC DEDCBAZO
X YZABCPQ RSTULOMNP
QUICKFLDELCFED GMI
H IJ KLMZBACDEFEGHG
QURSTU VU ST U V XYZAD
EFGHIJF DECBXAXABFI

DEFGLMNOABC
MNO LOLOQRST
YPDL PYLYPD PDQ
B C DESUTVDC EI
MNPOROMSRTU
ZXBACJ MJKEEGF
LMPO ZAB CADA
DFIEJLMKNCSTR
UPIRLFDE FNERR
DELFGHABC XYZ
JKOI MOSOCXOX
Q SRTGHIJIXYL

Pinprick code

Read all about how yesterday's newspaper can be used to conceal today's news!

What you need

Yesterday's newspaper (make sure everyone has finished reading it first!)

Piece of thick cardboard

Pin

What you do

1. Flick through the newspaper until you find an article with an interesting headline. Make a note of the headline.

2. Place the cardboard behind the article.

3. Now, working through the article line by line, carefully make tiny pinpricks underneath letters to spell out a message. For example, if your message is 'pinprick marks' find the first 'p', make a mark underneath, then the next 'i' etc., like this:

'IT'S UNBREAKABLE,' SAYS CHAMPION CODE BREAKER

This week, the British Superspy Headquarters announced that they were totally bewildered, baffled and bamboozled by a new code currently used by junior spies to send messages to each other.

Experts believe that newspapers hold the key to this complex code. But they haven't a clue how the code works...

When interviewed, super code breaker, Ms I Solvdit commented, 'It's unbreakable. The country's best brains have failed to crack this cunning code. We can only hope that the brilliant minds behind the newspaper code decide to work for us when they are old enough to leave school.'

4. To pass on this message to your code partner, just hand over the entire newspaper and whisper the headline of the article you pinpointed to them.

7080583 CRACK 7 THE 3 CODE 46356252

You'll need sharp eyes to spot the secret message in this page...

MYSTERIOUS MESSAGES FROM SPACE

An observatory in Hawaii, USA, has been receiving signals from an unknown source – some believe them to be messages from outer space. Code-breaking teams across the globe are listening to the signals to see if they can find any clues to the signals' meaning.

SPY CHIEF QUITS

A secret code-breaking unit has lost its chief of staff. For fear of being exposed by a national paper, M (as he is known) was forced to quit. 'Naming him would have threatened the whole operation,' said the Defence Minister. 'This would have been disastrous for national and international security.' Remarkably the vacant post has now been filled by an eighteen-year-old boy who is said to be a 'genius of the like never seen before in code-breaking circles'.

SECRET SPY SUPPLIES - **for all your spying needs**

Now in stock:

Classic spy macs • False-bottomed briefcases • fake ID (printed while you wait) • hollow walking sticks (room for 10 secret messages inside) • invisible ink

You'll find our shop at: ah, well... that's top secret

37486967080583463562526288949

Cracking facts!

Leonardo da Vinci (1452-1519) could turn his hand to just about anything. As well as painting the *Mona Lisa* – he was an expert engineer, a sculptor and a skilled anatomist. However, he had another less well-known talent: da Vinci was exceptionally good at mirror writing.

He didn't just do this every now and again – da Vinci filled page after page with mirror writing, even making scientific notes and labelling diagrams in this way. Many people have tried to guess why da Vinci did this. Was it because he was left-handed? (It is said to be much easier for left-handed people to write in this way). Did he want to keep his ideas secret? (Even though it is not very difficult to decode mirror writing...) Or maybe he just liked writing this way!

—•—•—•—•—•—•—

Lovestruck **Victorians** used to send messages to each other in the personal columns of newspapers, but they would encode their romantic words in case anyone else read them!

—•—•—•—•—•—•—

Mary Queen of Scots (1542-87) spent many years of her life as a prisoner of Queen Elizabeth I, who was worried that the Scottish queen wanted to steal her throne. To communicate with the captive queen, her supporters sent coded messages...

Unfortunately, messages sent to and from Mary were intercepted... by Elizabeth's spies. An expert code breaker revealed the meaning behind the strange symbols. Mary's supporters planned to rescue the Scottish queen and kill Elizabeth, so Mary was beheaded in 1587 – all because her code was cracked.

Chapter 10

INVISIBLE CODES

The code that is the most difficult to crack is the code that cannot even be seen.

Invisible ink

To make a message doubly secret, choose one of the codes in this book and then write in invisible ink... You don't need to mix together nasty, toxic, explosive chemicals to make invisible ink – sorry! In fact, you've probably already got some ready-to-use ink in your kitchen.

What you need

Half a lemon
Small bowl or eggcup
Small paintbrush
Paper
Adult with an iron!

What you do

1. Squeeze the lemon juice into a small bowl or an eggcup.

2. Use the paintbrush just like an old-fashioned quill pen. Dip it into the lemon juice and then write a secret message on the paper. Keep the paintbrush wet by dipping it into the juice every few letters.

3. When the ink is dry – be patient, it might take a few minutes – deliver your note!

4. To turn the invisible words into visible words, you'll need your adult. Ask him or her to put the paper on to an ironing

board, place a pillowcase over the top and then iron the pillowcase. When the pillowcase is removed, the message should have appeared. If it hasn't, ask your adult to iron for a few seconds longer. (Warning: do not attempt this on your own!)

Orange Juice, grapefruit Juice
and onion Juice also make
terrific invisible ink

Read between the lines!

Your enemies might think it strange if you send a blank piece of paper to a friend. To avoid them becoming suspicious, write a false message on to the paper using real ink. Then write the real message between the lines with invisible ink. If anyone intercepts the note, they'll only see one message!

Dent code

This is a form of secret writing that will make a real impression on code crackers everywhere!

What you need

Pencil sharpener
Hard-leaded pencil (2H)
Notebook
Soft-leaded pencil (2B)

What you do

1. Sharpen your 2H pencil to make sure that it has a really pointy tip.

2. Then write your message on to the top page of the notebook, making sure you press down hard. Be careful, though. You don't want to snap the pencil lead.

3. Now throw away this page. The next page in the notebook is the one that contains the secret message!

4. To reveal the secret writing, use the 2B pencil to scribble lightly all over the page. The dents that were made when the words were written on to the page above will show up as white writing, as on the next page.

The sharper your pencil and the harder
you press with it, the clearer your
message will be when it is revealed!

Watermark code

If you hold top-quality writing paper in front of a window or a light, you might see a pattern on it – this is a watermark. Here's how to write your own secret watermark words.

What you need

2 pieces of paper
Sink filled with water
Blunt pencil

What you do

1. Dip one sheet of paper into the sink and then place it on a hard, smooth surface. A kitchen worktop would be ideal.

2. Put the second sheet of paper on top of the wet sheet. Write your message on the dry sheet, pressing very firmly, then throw it away.

3. When you look at the wet sheet, you should be able to see the words that you've just written... But, as the sheet dries, the watermark writing will vanish completely!

4. The only way to reveal your message is to dip the sheet into water once again.

When watermark writing dries, it's totally invisible – even when the sheet of paper is held up to the light!

Torchlight code

Keep your enemies in the dark with secret writing that is invisible in daylight.

What you need

Two pieces of paper
Pen or sharp hard pencil
Torch

What you do

1. Place one sheet of paper on top of the other, then write your message on the top sheet pressing hard. Throw the top sheet away – your secret message is on the remaining sheet of paper.

2. To read the message, you must wait until night-time...

3. When it's dark, put the piece of paper on a flat surface.

4. Now, hold the torch beside the paper, so that its light is shining across the paper, not straight down on to it. You should now be able to read the message!

The slanted light from the torch shows up the marks pressed into the paper.

Milky ink

Use this invisible ink to add a bit of spice to your secret messages!

What you need

Splash of milk
Small bowl or eggcup
Small paintbrush
Paper
Cinnamon powder

What you do

1. Pour the milk into the bowl or eggcup. A teaspoon or two is more than enough.

2. Dip the paintbrush into the milk, then use it to paint a secret message on to the paper. You may need to dip the brush into the milk after painting each letter.

3. When the ink is dry, the message will have vanished.

4. To make the writing appear once more, shake a small amount of cinnamon on to the page.

5. Rubbing very lightly with your fingertip, smooth the cinnamon powder all over the page. Now tip the loose powder away (making sure you clear it up!).

6. As if by magic, the secret message will appear!

Cracking facts!

One special type of invisible ink can be seen only when ultraviolet light is shone on to it. The ink glows brightly to reveal the secret message. Unfortunately, this type of light also shows up things like fluff and dandruff...

There are two main types of invisible ink. One is revealed when chemicals are applied to the paper the message is written upon. The other becomes visible when the paper is heated. It is vital that each ink is made visible using the correct technique – otherwise, it could be destroyed. During the **American Revolution**, British spies avoided this problem by marking their letters with either an F (for fire) or an A (for acid) to show how hidden messages should be revealed.

If spies ever run out of invisible ink, it doesn't mean that they won't be able to write any more secret messages. They can use their own urine instead!

Chapter 11
Decoded!

All the answers to all of the CRACK THE CODE questions – revealed!

Shhhhh!

Both NVVG NV ZG MLLM and 13-5-5-20 13-5 1-20 14-15-15-14 mean:

MEET ME AT NOON

Chapter 1 SCRAMBLED CODES

Page 6 **Double Dutch**

CLOGS

CANALS

WINDMILL

AMSTERDAM

Page 8 **X-code**

THE NETHERLANDS

A LITTLE MOUSE WITH CLOGS ON

EDAM CHEESE IS REALLY TASTY

FLAT COUNTRIES ARE GOOD FOR BICYCLES

Page 9 ***Double-double Dutch***

NONSENSE

GIBBERISH

BALDERDASH

GOBBLEDYGOOK

Page 10 ***Sdrawkcab code***

BACK-TO-FRONT

ESPERANTO*

LOOK BEHIND YOU!

PUTTING THE CART BEFORE THE HORSE

* Esperanto is an artificial international language that was invented in 1887. It was hoped that Esperanto would be spoken by people from many different countries, leading to better communication around the world. It never caught on. (How many people speak it now?)

Page 11 ***Anagrams***

CODE WORD

CRACK THE CODE

SECRET MESSAGE

PUFFIN BOOKS

Chapter 2 SYMBOL CODES

Page 15 ***Number-cruncher code***

BINGO

LUCKY NUMBER

ONE TWO, BUCKLE MY SHOE

ONE TWO THREE FOUR FIVE, ONCE I CAUGHT A FISH ALIVE

Page 17 ***Criss-cross code***

Dear MAD HATTER

I was LOOKING FORWARD to being INVITED to your TEA PARTY. However, no INVITATION has ARRIVED. This is very RUDE and totally UNACCEPTABLE. I am very VERY CROSS.

From

ALICE (in WONDERLAND)

PS I shall probably COME ALONG anyway!

Page 18 ***Pigpen cipher***

THE PIGPEN CIPHER WAS USED DURING THE AMERICAN CIVIL WAR

Page 21 ***Semaphore code***

HELP

COME HERE

I AM HUNGRY

MY ARMS ARE TIRED

Page 23 ***Morse code***

COME AT ONCE. WE HAVE STRUCK AN ICEBERG.

RMS TITANIC

Chapter 3 KEYPAD CODES

Page 27 ***Telephone code***

CALL ME

RING RING

GIVE ME A BELL

SMILE BEFORE YOU DIAL

Page 29 ***Mobile shorthand***

HIGH FIVE

ARE YOU OK?

BE SEEING YOU, MATE!

SEE YOU LATER FOR TENNIS

Page 31 ***Keyboard code***

QWERTY KEYBOARDS

THE LETTERS ON YOUR COMPUTER KEYBOARD ARE IN THE SAME ORDER AS THOSE ON THE FIRST TYPEWRITER – INVENTED OVER A HUNDRED YEARS AGO. IT IS CALLED A QWERTY KEYBOARD BECAUSE Q, W, E, R, T AND Y ARE THE FIRST SIX LETTERS ON THE TOP ROW.

Page 33 ***Keyboard hieroglyphics***

A MUMMY'S CURSE

THE EGYPTIAN SPHINX

THE VALLEY OF THE KINGS

THE GREAT PYRAMID OF GIZA

Chapter 4 WORD CODES

Page 37 **Acrostic code**

PURPLE (read down the first letters of each line)

ENIGMA (read up the last letters of each line)

Page 39 **Missing-word code**

CRACK THE CODE (fifth word)

SEE YOU AT FIVE (fifth word)

MY MIDDLE NAME IS ALGERNON (sixth word)

TREASURE IS IN THE WOODEN CHEST (eighth word)

Page 41 **Book code**

'The sly brown fox jumped quickly over the lazy dog' is a very special sentence. It contains all the letters of the alphabet!

Page 43 **Cookery code**

The code words are highlighted below.
Two things **you'll** need are an apron and a rolling pin.
For (4!) a successful recipe, **have** your oven nice and hot before you start cooking.

3 satsumas or **a** navel orange

2 cups **really** hot water

2 carrots (**grate** one of them)

2 teaspoons **thyme**

1 **cooking** apple

So, the coded message is: You'll have a really grate thyme (great time) cooking.

Page 44-45 ***Bookworm code***

MY DIARY IS PRIVATE

TIME: FOUR
PLACE: SCHOOL GATES

I WANT TO BE A DJ
(The number 2345 at the beginning of the last title means that you should use the second, third, fourth and fifth words.)

COME TO MY HOUSE AT SIX

Chapter 5 LETTER CODES

Page 49 ***Shopping-list code***

SUPERMARKET

SHOE SHOP

GREENGROCER

TRAVEL AGENT

Page 51 ***Telephone-number code***

MOBILE PHONE

DIALLING TONE

DOG AND BONE (Rhyming slang for TELEPHONE)

VIDEOPHONE

Page 53 ***First-letter code***

HURRY

PASSWORD MAUVE

SEE YOU AT 5

COME TO THE CINEMA

Page 54 ***Fifth-letter code***

SQUARE

TRIANGLE

HEXAGON (a six-sided shape)

DODECAHEDRON (a twelve-sided shape)

Page 55 ***Riddle code***

My first is in rich – R

My second is in ditch – I

My third is in code – D

My fourth is in toad – D

My fifth is in myrtle – L

My sixth is in purple – E

The word is RIDDLE

Chapter 6 GRID CODES

Page 59 ***Up-and-down code***

JACK IN THE BOX

PUPPET ON A STRING

SNAKES AND LADDERS

A LIFE ON THE OCEAN WAVES

Page 61 ***Zigzag code***

WIGGLY ROAD

CROOKED PATH

TWISTS AND TURNS

UPSTAIRS AND DOWNSTAIRS

Page 63 ***Twisted code***

MERRY GO ROUND

HELTER SKELTER

THE WORM HAS TURNED

LET'S TWIST AGAIN

Page 65 ***Spiralling code***

WHIRLPOOL

WHIRLIGIG

SPIRAL STAIRCASE

A TORNADO IS COMING

Page 67 ***Odd-and-even code***

ODD ONE OUT

SHUFFLE THE LETTERS

ONE THREE FIVE SEVEN NINE

TWO FOUR SIX EIGHT TEN TWELVE

Chapter 7 SWAP CODES

Page 71 ***ZYX code***

ALPHABET

TWENTY-SIX LETTERS

IT'S AS EASY AS ABC

DICTIONARIES LIST WORDS IN ALPHABETICAL ORDER

Page 73 ***Shift code***

BUDGE UP

MOVE SIDEWAYS

TAKE A STEP TO THE LEFT

USE THE NEXT LETTER IN THE ALPHABET

Page 75 ***Multiple-shift code***

JULIUS CAESAR

LEWIS CARROLL

BLAISE DE VIGNERE

SIR ARTHUR CONAN DOYLE

Page 77 ***Random-letter code***

Chapter 8 GADGET CODES

Page 85 ***Grille code***

It is said that Cardinal RICHELIEU used a grille to encode and decode secret messages in the 1600s.

Page 89 ***Code Wheel***

SPINNING WHEEL

ROUND AND ROUND

WHEELY FAB

GOING ROUND IN CIRCLES

Page 91 ***Paperclip code***

DO NOT LET THE PAPERCLIP FALL INTO ENEMY HANDS!

Page 93 ***Ruler code***

CENTIMETRE

ONE TWO THREE FOUR FIVE

A LONG STRAIGHT MESSAGE

MEASURE FOR MEASURE

Chapter 9 CUNNING CODES

Page 97 **Mirror code**

MIRROR MIRROR ON THE WALL

THROUGH THE LOOKING-GLASS

LEONARDO DA VINCI (See page 110 for a cracking fact about the famous artist!)

NARCISSUS FELL IN LOVE WITH HIS OWN REFLECTION

Page 98 **See-through code**

THIS CODE IS COOL (page 98)

TOP SECRET MESSAGES CAN BE HIDDEN IN YOUR FAVOURITE BOOKS (page 100)

Page 103 **Crossword code**

CROSSWORD

SOLVE IT

CONUNDRUM (another word for 'puzzle')

CRACK THE CODES

Page 105 **Origami code**

EMERGENCY MEETING AT ONCE

FOLD A NOTE TO KEEP IT SECRET

CRACK THE CREASED CODE

FOLD PAPER FIRMLY TO MAKE A SHARP CREASE

Page 107 ***Pinprick code***

CODED MESSAGES ARE EASILY HIDDEN